DIEHARD CARDS

ST. LOUIS CARDINALS 2006 WORLD SERIES CHAMPIONS

Edited by Doug Hoepker

Foreword by Larry Borowsky

SP
SPORTS
PUBLISHING
L.L.C.

SportsPublishingLLC.com

ISBN 10: 1-59670-239-7 (Soft Cover)
ISBN 13: 978-1-59670-239-4 (Soft Cover)

ISBN 10: 1-59670-238-9 (Hard Cover)
ISBN 13: 978-1-59670-238-7 (Hard Cover)

© 2006 Doug Hoepker and Larry Borowsky

Front cover: Albert Pujols photograph—Victor Baldizon/Getty Images; 2006 World Series photogaph—Elsa/Getty Images. Back cover: 2006 World Series photograph—Jed Jacobsohn/Getty Images.

SportsPublishingLLC.com

Publishers: Peter L. Bannon and Joseph J. Bannon Sr.
Senior managing editor: Susan M. Moyer
Editor: Doug Heopker
Art director: K. Jeffrey Higgerson
Photo editor: Erin Linden-Levy
Cover design: Joseph Brumleve
Graphic design: K. Jeffrey Higgerson

Sports Publishing L.L.C.
804 North Neil Street
Champaign, IL 61820
Phone: 1-877-424-2665
Fax: 217-363-2073
SportsPublishingLLC.com

Printed in the United States of America.

FOREWORD

By Larry Borowsky

I keep coming back to the foul balls.

Twenty-six of them, all with two strikes; all hit by the Cardinals in Game 2 of the National League Championship Series against the New York Mets. Twenty-six diehard swings; 26 refusals to get beat and take a seat on the bench. The Cardinals trailed for most of that game, and they spent most of the night batting from behind in the count.

But that hardly fazed these guys. It seemed like they'd had two strikes against them for months.

A season that began with high hopes had gone horribly awry. Injuries, late-inning losses, and long losing streaks marred the summer, knocking the Cardinals off the 100-win perch they had occupied the previous two years. A seven-game skid in late September cost the Cardinals nearly all of their large lead in the NL Central standings and brought them to the brink of a humiliating collapse. They hung on to clinch the division on the last day of the season, but the Cards limped into the playoffs with an 83-78 record, the third-weakest mark of any postseason team in history. The pundits wrote them off; even their own fans didn't hold out much hope.

Despite a first-round playoff triumph over the San Diego Padres, the Cardinals were prohibitive underdogs in the NLCS to the powerful Mets, whose 97-65 record was tied for the best in baseball in 2006. New York asserted itself in Game 1 with a convincing 2-0 victory, then opened Game 2 by bruising St. Louis ace Chris Carpenter for three quick runs. The Mets appeared ready to blow the series open, but the Cardinals refused to go quietly. Leading off the top of the second, Jim Edmonds fouled off a 3-2 pitch—the first of those 26 two-strike fouls—and drew a walk, sparking a two-run rally to get the Cards back into the game. In the third, Albert Pujols fouled off two full-count pitches before drawing ball four; Edmonds immediately followed with a game-tying homer. In the seventh, with the Cardinals trailing again, Pujols fouled off *five* 3-2 pitches from Mets reliever Guillermo Mota, finally lining a fastball—the 11th pitch of the at-bat—into left field for a single to spark another game-tying rally.

Diehard Cards, indeed.

Adam Wainwright (No. 50) and his St. Louis teammates celebrate after the final out of the 2006 World Series. Jonathan Daniel/Getty Images

So Taguchi led off the ninth inning with the score still tied and promptly fell behind in the count 0-2 against New York closer Billy Wagner. He ripped one foul, took a few pitches, worked the count full, then fouled back a couple more. Taguchi was taking full cuts, not holding anything back; if he went down, at least he was going to do it swinging. Wagner's ninth pitch was a fastball over the outside corner, 95-plus miles per hour; but Taguchi had him timed by now. He flung his bat head around and smoked a laser beam over the fence—and the tone of the series had suddenly, irrevocably shifted. The Diehard Cards were very much alive; after Game 2, St. Louis would never again face a series deficit throughout the postseason.

None of those 26 two-strike foul balls drove in a run or showed up on an ESPN high-light reel. They merely fended off outs, kept batters alive, and prolonged a game the Cardinals could not afford to lose.

Above all, they gave an imperfect team one more chance to get it right.

In truth, the Cardinals had been trying to to get it right since 2004, when they reached the World Series for the first time in Tony La Russa's managerial tenure. Their four-game sweep that year at the hands of the Boston Red Sox left the franchise and its fans hungry for redemption. But a 100-win season in 2005 ended just short of the Series; the Cardinals succumbed to the Houston Astros in the NLCS, four games to two, leaving the bad memories of 2004 to linger for at least one more season.

They followed the Cardinals to a new ballpark in 2006: Busch Stadium III. Already half-built by the end of the 2005 season, the new stadium was completed just in time for Opening Day 2006. Busch III's footprint overlapped with that of the old stadium, symbolizing the continuity of tradition—in a sense, the Cards were still playing on the same grounds that had witnessed two world titles and six National League pennants. The sparkling new building was almost as big an attraction as the ballclub itself—a good chunk of the schedule sold out before a single pitch had been thrown, and standing-room-only crowds packed the house almost nightly.

Work continued at Busch III until almost Memorial Day, as the left-field grandstand was completed. Construction of the Cardinal roster, meanwhile, continued well beyond that. Throughout 2006, the ballclub remained a work in progress—chunks of the façade were constantly crumbling, forcing La Russa and general manager Walt Jocketty to rebuild and reinforce. The projected starters at two positions didn't even break camp with the team: Second baseman Junior Spivey batted .138 in spring training and spent the whole season at Triple A, while injury-plagued left fielder Larry Bigbie started only four games all year. Relief pitcher Ricardo Rincon left in April to have season-ending elbow surgery; Scott Rolen missed nearly two weeks with a viral condition; and starting pitchers Sidney Ponson and Chris Carpenter made trips to the disabled list in mid-May. Centerfielder Jim Edmonds struggled all spring with shoulder and abdominal ailments; he reached Memorial Day with just five home runs, 29 RBIs, and a .241 batting average.

With so many players missing or injured, La Russa had to put some makeshift teams on the field. But every lineup seemed to produce as long as it included one name: Pujols. The defending National League Most Valuable Player proved himself more than

Tony La Russa celebrates with Yadier Molina after the completion of the NLCS at Shea Stadium. Jim McIsaac/Getty Images

worthy of the title in the first half of 2006. He seemed at times to be a one-man team, singlehandedly turning defeats into Cardinal victories. Albert homered twice on Opening Day at Philadelphia, then launched a missile in the home opener—the first Cardinal homer in Busch Stadium III. A few days later he pounded *three* homers, the last of which erased a one-run deficit in the bottom of the ninth and gave St. Louis an 8-7 walkoff win over the Reds. Albert finished April with 14 homers, an all-time record for the month.

As late as Memorial Day, Pujols was on pace for 80 homers and nearly 200 RBIs. Thanks largely to him, the Cardinals reached the end of May with the best record in the National League and the second-best record in baseball (behind the Tigers). Then, on June 3 in a nationally televised game against the Cubs, the unthinkable occurred: Pujols left with an injury. He'd strained his right oblique and had to go onto the disabled list for the first time in his career. It was the first real challenge for the Diehard Cards, and they proved themselves up to the test. Scott Rolen, back healthy from the shoulder woes that sidelined him for most of 2005, took over the No. 3 slot in the batting order and drove in 16 runs. New right-fielder Juan Encarnacion batted .441. Rookie Chris Duncan, called up to take Pujols' roster spot, slugged .571 in part-time duty. With admirable courage, the Cards maintained their lead atop the NL Central in the absence of their premiere player—the first indication of how this group of players would react in a crisis.

Unfortunately, it was not the last crisis they would face. While Pujols convalesced, another injury announced itself forcefully: Mark Mulder's left shoulder. On the same day Albert hurt himself, the Cubs had pounded Mulder for 12 hits and eight runs, the left-hander's second straight eight-run outing. He would make three more starts after that, each more painfully ineffective than the last; in his final one, against the White Sox on June 20, he gave up nine runs in just 2 $\frac{1}{3}$ innings, sending the Cards to an embarrassing 20-6 loss. The next day Mulder followed Pujols to the DL, his season essentially over. In his absence, rotation depth—perhaps the greatest asset of the Cards' back-to-back 100-win teams—became a summer-long problem in St. Louis. After finishing among the top two in team ERA in 2004-05, the Cards would stumble to ninth place in that category in 2006.

The 20-6 loss at Comiskey launched the Cardinals' longest losing streak in nearly two decades—eight games. That jarring development served ample notice that the 2006 Cardinals were not the same juggernaut that had steamrolled the competition the previous two years. Adjusting on the fly, La Russa turned left field over to rookie Chris Duncan and moved rookie Anthony Reyes into the starting rotation. Although fans (and some Cardinal players) hoped for an "impact" acquisition at the trade deadline, Jocketty couldn't find the right partner; he did bring in Jeff Weaver to reinforce the pitching staff and Ron Belliard to play second base, while Preston Wilson and Jose Vizcaino added bench depth. But the core of the team would have to stand or fall on its own.

In late July a freak weather front blew through downtown St. Louis right before a ball-game. Gale-force winds ripped through the Busch III concourses, a perfect symbol for the state of the Cardinals—stormy. The players were frustrated, the fans impatient; although the new stadium continued to sell out night after night, boos rained down on the home team with depressing regularity. In late July the Cardinals went on a second eight-game losing streak, which so dispirited La Russa that he walked out of the postgame press conference after one loss with barely a word to the media.

Through it all, the Diehard Cards remained in first place. They stayed there even after Edmonds went out with post-concussion syndrome and shortstop David Eckstein went down for six weeks with a strained oblique (the same injury that had sidelined Pujols). Another blow fell in September, when Jason Isringhausen finally succumbed to a sore hip that had been bothering him for months. The Cards' normally reliable closer hadn't been himself all season, losing more games in 2006 alone (eight) than in his previous four years as a Cardinal combined. On September 7 Izzy shut it down for the season, destabilizing the bullpen and nearly causing the wobbly Cards to collapse entirely. After his departure, St. Louis lost eight games in their opponents' final at-bat, including five in which they held a lead after the seventh inning.

The bullpen's struggles contributed to one final losing streak, seven games long, that brought the Cardinals to the brink of an historic collapse. In the span of nine days, their lead over the Astros shriveled from seven and a half games to a mere half-game. The media began comparing the Cards to the infamous 1964 Phillies, the epic chokers of baseball lore. But with history and injuries and the onrushing Astros weighing upon them, the Diehard Cards refused to give in. They clinched on the final day of the season and returned to the playoffs for the sixth time in seven years.

The Cardinals had begun 2006 in a new stadium built atop the rubble of the old. They ended it by constructing a new season upon the fallen hopes and wrecked expectations of a lackluster regular season. The Cardinals took a wrecking ball to their 83-78 record, tore it down and threw the blueprints out the window. In the postseason they reconstituted themselves as a sturdier, more unshakeable team—one designed to withstand the difficult tests of October.

In a very real sense, the Cardinals' regular-season struggles laid a solid foundation for postseason success. The players were battle-tested, inured to pressure; they confronted make-or-break playoff situations fearlessly. More important, the Cardinals of October were generally healthy. Edmonds and Eckstein, available for just a handful of games apiece in September, started every playoff game. The Cards' three ablest starting pitchers—Chris Carpenter, Jeff Suppan, and Jeff Weaver—took the ball for 14 of the team's 16 October games. And La Russa, having spent most of September sorting

Albert Pujols (with his son, A.J.), Bill DeWitt, Walt Jocketty, and Tony La Russa hold the World Series trophy. Elise Amendola-Pool/Getty Images

out new bullpen roles in the post-Isringhausen era, finally tabbed three rookies as his late-inning specialists: Josh Kinney and Tyler Johnson as set-up men, Adam Wainwright in Izzy's old job as closer. Together with southpaw specialist Randy Flores (who also handled some late-inning assignments), the young bullpenners allowed only one run in 29 October innings.

The Cards started the October tournament on the road, where they had compiled a flimsy .420 winning percentage in 2006, and pounded out two convincing wins over the Padres. After finishing off that series in four games, the Cardinals confronted the mighty Mets and battled them toe to toe for six games. In an epic Game 7, Jeff Suppan and the

Mets' Oliver Perez battled each other to a 1-1 draw through seven breathless innings; the bullpens took over in the eighth, and the Cardinals broke through on a shocking two-run homer by Yadier Molina with one out in the ninth inning. But before unfurling the pennant, the Cardinals had to survive a heart-stopping showdown with Carlos Beltran with two outs and the bases loaded in the bottom of the ninth. Beltran, who nearly beat the Cardinals single-handedly as a member of the Astros in the 2004 NLCS, had plagued them again in 2006. He came to the plate with seven career postseason homers against St. Louis. An eighth, and the pennant would fly above Shea Stadium; an out, and the Cardinals would carry it off. Thoughts of all those late-inning September losses flashed through every Cardinal fan's mind. ... But this wasn't September. Wainwright didn't flinch. He got ahead with a fastball, threw a curve for strike two, and then paralyzed Beltran with another curve that traced a gorgeous arc over the outer half of the plate. That pitch was like the final blow of the wrecking ball, toppling a season's worth of frustrations: the Diehard Cards were NL champions. They were heading back to the World Series.

Nobody gave them much of a chance to beat the American League champion Detroit Tigers. But they split the first two in Detroit, won Game 3 on a Carpenter shutout, then staged a stirring come-from-behind win in Game 4. And in Game 5, they clinched the title with a 4-2 win behind Jeff Weaver—a perfect symbol for a team that wouldn't quit. Discarded by the Angels after going 3-10 with a 6.20 era, Weaver hung in there during a rocky first month with the Cardinals; he heard boos at Busch Stadium in August during a blowout loss to Philadelphia. But as he walked off after eight strong innings against Detroit in Game 5, he heard nothing but appreciative cheers.

The Diehard Cards had survived. And in the process, they'd buried the disappointments of World Series past—laid them to rest alongside the dearly departed Busch Stadium II. The rebuilt team in the newly built ballpark gave St. Louis its 10th, and most improbable, world championship.

Larry Borowsky writes Viva El Birdos *(www.vivaelbirdos.com), a blog about the St. Louis Cardinals. He has written about the Cardinals for* Slate, *the* Wall Street Journal Online, Baseball Analysts, *and other Web sites.*

APRIL

Expectations ran high for the St. Louis Cardinals entering the 2006 season. Coming off two-straight 100-win seasons and two crushing postseason defeats, fans wanted to see an energized, rebuilt team storm out of the gate and claim what was rightfully theirs: a World Series title. GM Walt Jocketty spent the off-season filling needs, and the '06 club featured new corner outfielders; a turnstile at second base; a revamped, relatively inexperienced bullpen; and a recently freed-from-jail starting pitcher. Fans concerned about the lack of a big-name free agent addition exercised cautious optimism. Yet, by the end of April, rooters were ready to toss caution to the wind. A franchise-best 17 wins in April delivered the team a share of first place with the Cincinnati Reds. More importantly, Albert Pujols was having a month for the ages. The slugger finished April with a Major League-record 14 home runs to go along with 32 RBIs and a .346 average. It was the start of something special.

Cardinals fans await the start of the first game at the new Busch Stadium. Albert Dickson/TSN/ZUMA Press/Icon SMI

Albert Pujols walked to lead off the ninth in a tied game. With Phillies clos-er Tom Gordon on the mound, Jim Edmonds struck out, but Pujols then stole second and advanced to third on the catcher's throwing error. Rolen ground-ed into a fielder's choice to short, with Jimmy Rollins throwing Pujols out at home. Now with two outs in the inning, Scott Schumaker walked, moving Rolen into scoring position. Yadier Molina followed with a two-out, game-winning single to left. In the bottom of the ninth, Jason Isringhausen worked out of a bases-loaded jam to get his first save of the year.

April 5
@ PHI
W, 4-3

April 7
@ CHC
L, 5-1

April 3
@ PHI
W, 13-5

April 6
@ PHI
W, 4-2

Cardinal great Stan Musial waves to the crowd during pregame Opening Day ceremonies. Rich Pilling/MLB Photos via Getty Images

One day after the bullpen blew the game by allowing home runs to Michael Barrett and Derek Lee, they did so again. The Cubs completed the sweep with an 8-4 win on the strength of a five-run eighth inning. Jason Isringhausen entered the game with a runner on first and no outs. He then walked the bases loaded and surrendered a grand slam to Barrett. The Cubs scored another run before the inning was through, and the Cardinals went quietly in the top of the ninth against Cubs closer Ryan Dempster.

**April 9
@ CHC
L, 8-4**

**April 12
MIL
W, 8-3**

**April 8
@ CHC
L, 3-2**

**April 10
MIL
W, 6-4**

Opening Day at the new Busch Stadium featured home runs from both predictable and unpredictable sources. After Brewers infielder Bill Hall connected for the first home run in Busch Stadium history in the second inning, Pujols hit the first Cardinals home run at the new park the following inning. Mark Mulder then hit his first career home run in the seventh inning to complement his fine day on the mound.

LEFT: Chris Carpenter pitches against Carlos Zambrano and the Chicago Cubs at Wrigley Field. Jonathan Daniel/Getty Images
BELOW: The St. Louis skyline, one of the key elements of the new Busch Stadium, is reflected in So Taguchi's helmet. AP/WWP

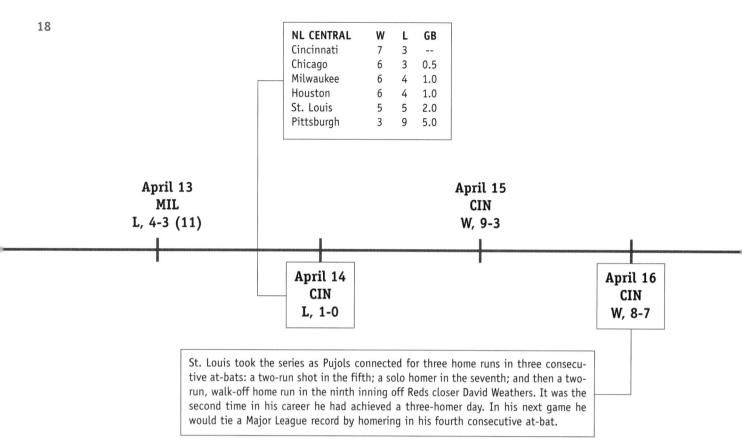

NL CENTRAL	W	L	GB
Cincinnati	7	3	--
Chicago	6	3	0.5
Milwaukee	6	4	1.0
Houston	6	4	1.0
St. Louis	5	5	2.0
Pittsburgh	3	9	5.0

April 13
MIL
L, 4-3 (11)

April 15
CIN
W, 9-3

April 14
CIN
L, 1-0

April 16
CIN
W, 8-7

St. Louis took the series as Pujols connected for three home runs in three consecutive at-bats: a two-run shot in the fifth; a solo homer in the seventh; and then a two-run, walk-off home run in the ninth inning off Reds closer David Weathers. It was the second time in his career he had achieved a three-homer day. In his next game he would tie a Major League record by homering in his fourth consecutive at-bat.

Mark Mulder takes a curtain call after hitting his first career homer, a two-run shot in the Cardinals home opener. AP/WWP

After his team yielded 15 hits to the Pirates the day before, Chris Carpenter rallied the Cardinals with a brilliant performance in which he surrendered just two hits and one walk in eight shutout innings. Jim Edmonds chipped in with his second home run of the season and three RBIs, and David Eckstein also hit his first homer of 2006.

April 17
@ PIT
W, 2-1

April 19
@ PIT
W, 4-0

April 18
@ PIT
L, 12-4

April 21
CHC
W, 9-3

Pujols became the second fastest player in Major League history to collect 1,000 hits when he smacked a two-run home run in the first inning. He later added a double and totaled four RBIs to give Mark Mulder, who pitched eight strong innings, all the offense he would need.

Scott Spiezio provided surprising punch for the Cardinals lineup as an occasional starter and pinchhitter. Elsa/Getty Images

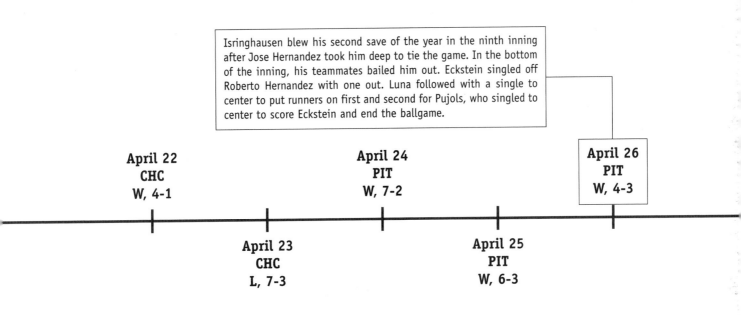

Isringhausen blew his second save of the year in the ninth inning after Jose Hernandez took him deep to tie the game. In the bottom of the inning, his teammates bailed him out. Eckstein singled off Roberto Hernandez with one out. Luna followed with a single to center to put runners on first and second for Pujols, who singled to center to score Eckstein and end the ballgame.

April 22
CHC
W, 4-1

April 23
CHC
L, 7-3

April 24
PIT
W, 7-2

April 25
PIT
W, 6-3

April 26
PIT
W, 4-3

LEFT: Albert Pujols celebrates after hitting his third home run in the game to beat the Reds on April 16, 2006. Elsa/Getty Images
BELOW: The Cardinals mob Albert Pujols after his game-winning homer against the Reds on April 16, 2006. Elsa/Getty Images

Pujols' month to remember ended in dramatic fashion as he hit his record-breaking 14th home run in April—a game-winner. Carpenter and Livan Hernandez locked up in a stingy pitcher's duel through seven innings. The difference in the game was each team's pen: St. Louis received two scoreless innings from Braden Looper and Isringhausen, but Nationals reliever Jon Rauch gave up the home run to Pujols. The following day the Cards posted their 17th win in the month of April, a new franchise record.

April 27
WAS
W, 6-2

April 29
WAS
W, 2-1

April 28
WAS
L, 8-3

April 30
WAS
W, 9-2

NL CENTRAL	W	L	GB
Cincinnati	17	8	--
St. Louis	17	8	--
Houston	16	8	0.5
Milwaukee	14	11	3.0
Chicago	13	10	3.0
Pittsburgh	7	19	10.5

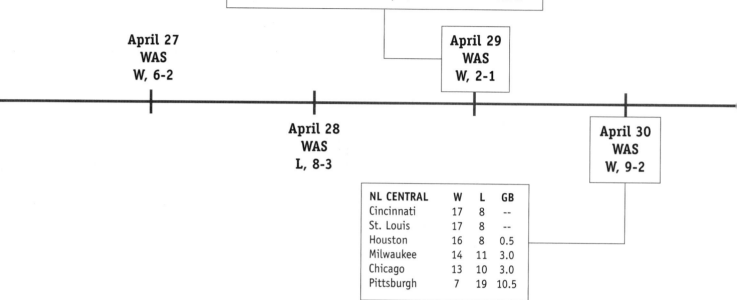

RIGHT: Juan Encarnacion makes a diving catch against the Pirates. Elsa/Getty Images
BELOW: Scott Rolen stretches to make the catch on a hit by the Phillies' Pat Burrell. AP/WWP

MAY

MAY

May began on a flat note as the Cardinals dropped four-straight games to the Reds and Astros, providing the first flash of the inconsistency that would plague the team all season long. They rebounded to win 14 of their next 17 games. Pujols continued his torrid pace—in one stretch homering in four consecutive at-bats to tie another Major League record—while the pitching staff maintained its ranking among the league's best. Mulder, considered by many to be a key part of the Cardinals rotation as its lone lefty, was looking sharp through mid-May with a 5-1 record and a 3.69 ERA. Newcomer Sidney Ponson battled through a minor injury in May to post a 4-0 mark and a 2.92 ERA. Things were looking up for the Redbirds, especially since third baseman Scott Rolen was hitting like his old All-Star self. Capping the month with a dramatic 4-3, 11-inning win over Houston, St. Louis entered June with an NL-best 34 wins and a five-game lead in the standings.

Young fans cheer for Albert Pujols during a game against the Rockies. AP/WWP

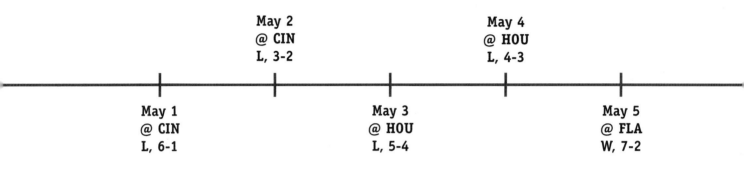

May 1
@ CIN
L, 6-1

May 2
@ CIN
L, 3-2

May 3
@ HOU
L, 5-4

May 4
@ HOU
L, 4-3

May 5
@ FLA
W, 7-2

Chris Duncan and his father, pitching coach Dave Duncan, chat before the Giants game. Michael Zagaris/MLB Photos via Getty Images

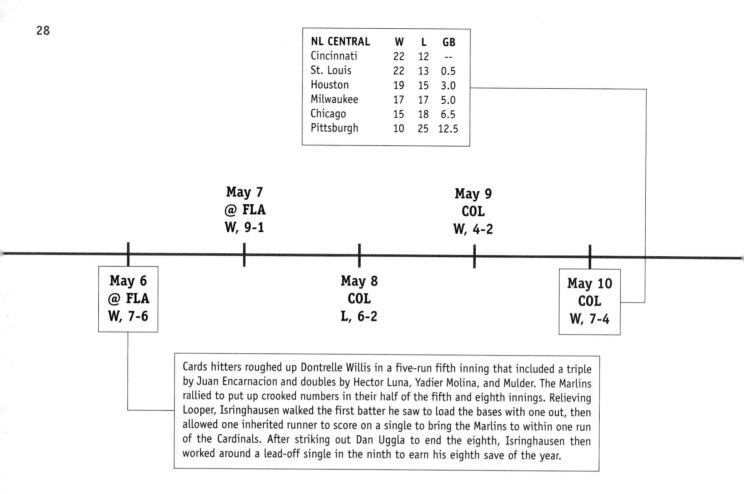

NL CENTRAL	W	L	GB
Cincinnati	22	12	--
St. Louis	22	13	0.5
Houston	19	15	3.0
Milwaukee	17	17	5.0
Chicago	15	18	6.5
Pittsburgh	10	25	12.5

May 7
@ FLA
W, 9-1

May 9
COL
W, 4-2

May 6
@ FLA
W, 7-6

May 8
COL
L, 6-2

May 10
COL
W, 7-4

Cards hitters roughed up Dontrelle Willis in a five-run fifth inning that included a triple by Juan Encarnacion and doubles by Hector Luna, Yadier Molina, and Mulder. The Marlins rallied to put up crooked numbers in their half of the fifth and eighth innings. Relieving Looper, Isringhausen walked the first batter he saw to load the bases with one out, then allowed one inherited runner to score on a single to bring the Marlins to within one run of the Cardinals. After striking out Dan Uggla to end the eighth, Isringhausen then worked around a lead-off single in the ninth to earn his eighth save of the year.

RIGHT: Hurdling Colorado's Cory Sullivan, David Eckstein turns the double play. Elsa/Getty Images
BELOW: Brad Thompson pitches in relief against the San Francisco Giants. Jed Jacobsohn/Getty Images

Mulder dominated the Mets, striking out five batters while tossing eight innings of four-hit ball. Rolen doubled in the sixth inning to score Pujols from first for the team's lone run.

May 12
ARI
W, 5-3

May 14
ARI
L, 7-6

May 17
NYM
W, 1-0

May 13
ARI
W, 9-1

May 16
NYM
L, 8-3

Cardinals hitters pounced on Diamondbacks starter Claudio Vargas: Pujols, Edmonds, and Rolen combined for seven hits, six runs, and nine RBIs. John Rodriguez, getting the start in left, went 3-for-5 with a double and two runs scored. Aaron Miles also had two hits on the day, keeping his batting average well above .300. Marquis pitched seven impressive innings, allowing just three hits and one earned run. Pujols stole the show with his home run, however, becoming the fastest player in Major League history to reach the 19-homer plateau in a season.

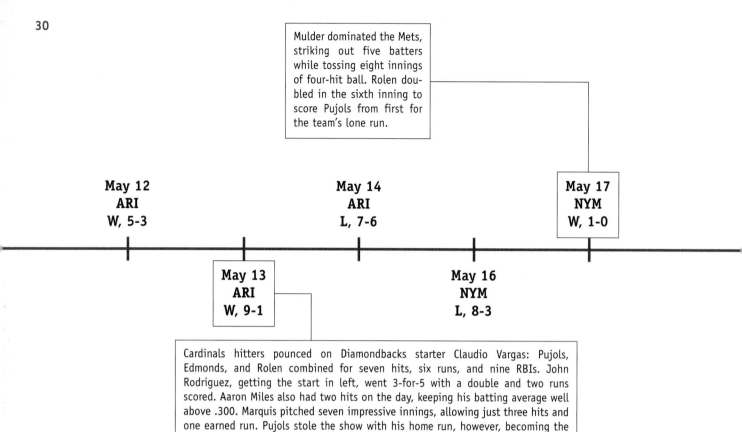

RIGHT: Scott Spiezio uses a pink bat in honor of Mother's Day and breast cancer survivors on May 14, 2006. Elsa/Getty Images
BELOW: Sidney Ponson exceeded expectations for the first two months of the 2006 season. John Grieshop/MLB Photos via Getty Images

NL CENTRAL	W	L	GB
St. Louis	29	16	--
Cincinnati	26	19	3.0
Houston	25	20	4.0
Milwaukee	23	22	6.0
Chicago	18	26	10.5
Pittsburgh	14	31	15.0

May 19
@ KAN
W, 9-6

May 21
@ KAN
W, 10-3

May 18
NYM
W, 6-3

May 20
@ KAN
W, 4-2

May 22
@ SFO
L, 9-2

Pujols, who homered in each game of this series, hit his 21st dinger of the year in Anthony Reyes' 2006 debut. Reyes worked 5 ⅔ innings, allowing four hits, one walk, and no runs. The following day, another key rookie, Chris Duncan, would make his first mark on the season, hitting his first home run of 2006.

Aaron Miles signs autographs before a May game against the Reds. John Grieshop/MLB Photos via Getty Images

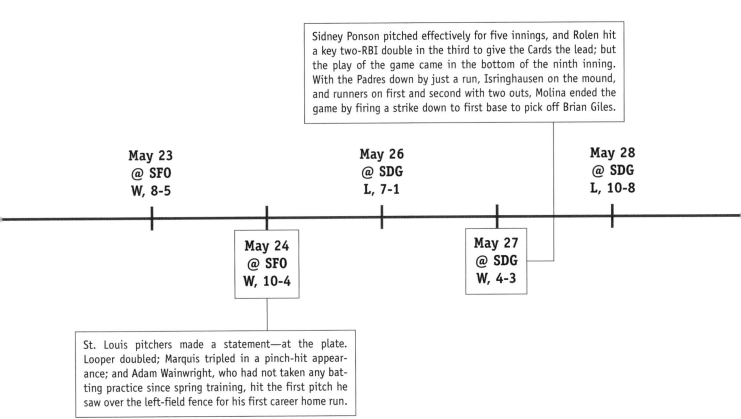

Sidney Ponson pitched effectively for five innings, and Rolen hit a key two-RBI double in the third to give the Cards the lead; but the play of the game came in the bottom of the ninth inning. With the Padres down by just a run, Isringhausen on the mound, and runners on first and second with two outs, Molina ended the game by firing a strike down to first base to pick off Brian Giles.

May 23
@ SFO
W, 8-5

May 26
@ SDG
L, 7-1

May 28
@ SDG
L, 10-8

May 24
@ SFO
W, 10-4

May 27
@ SDG
W, 4-3

St. Louis pitchers made a statement—at the plate. Looper doubled; Marquis tripled in a pinch-hit appearance; and Adam Wainwright, who had not taken any batting practice since spring training, hit the first pitch he saw over the left-field fence for his first career home run.

Yadier Molina, Chris Duncan, and John Rodriguez look on from the dugout. Michael Zagaris/MLB Photos via Getty Images

St. Louis won a nerve-racking 11-inning game after Wainwright, Isringhausen, and Looper combined to pitch five scoreless innings in relief of Jeff Suppan. In the 11th, Molina doubled to deep center field with one out. Miles reached on an infield single; after Luna lined out, Eckstein was hit by a pitch to load the bases for So Taguchi, who singled in the winning run.

May 29
HOU
W, 3-1

May 31
HOU
W, 4-3 (11)

May 30
HOU
L, 6-3

RIGHT: *Yadier Molina waits to take the field against the San Francisco Giants.* Michael Zagaris/MLB Photos via Getty Images
BELOW: *After scoring a run, Jim Edmonds is congratulated by his teammates.* Paul Jasienski/Getty Images

JUNE

JUNE

What a difference one month can make. Cardinals fans felt invincible on June 1, but by June 30, they were awakened by a whole new reality: The 2006 season would not be a cakewalk. An eight-game losing streak—the longest Cardinals skid since 1988—featured embarrassing defeats to American League powerhouses Chicago and Detroit. In just two games against the defending world champs, St. Louis pitchers surrendered 40 hits, eight home runs, and 33 runs. Concussions sustained by Eckstein and Edmonds were but minor distractions from the medical news on everyone's mind: When would Pujols return from a strained right oblique muscle, and would he be the same once he did? Pujols answered both of those questions with startling retorts. Doctors said he could be out a month or longer, but a determined Pujols was back in the lineup after missing just 15 games. In his second game back, he went 4-for-4 with a home run. With Albert cured, it was time to focus on what ailed the team.

RIGHT: Anthony Reyes pitched a dazzling one-hitter against the White Sox on June 22, 2006. AP/WWP
BELOW: Cardinals fans were wondering where the charge had gone in their team during an eight-game skid in June. AP/WWP

NL CENTRAL	W	L	GB
St. Louis	35	22	--
Cincinnati	33	24	2.0
Milwaukee	27	31	8.5
Houston	27	31	8.5
Chicago	23	33	11.5
Pittsburgh	22	36	13.5

June 3
CHC
L, 8-5

June 5
CIN
L, 8-7

June 2
CHC
L, 5-4 (14)

June 4
CHC
W, 9-6

Rolen had a key two-RBI double in the seventh to give St. Louis the lead, but later coughed up the lead himself on an uncharacteristic error in the top of the ninth when a ground ball passed through his legs. With the game tied in extra innings, the Cardinals failed to score despite loading the bases in the tenth and 12th innings. In the top of the 14th, Josh Hancock could not work around a lead-off double to Juan Pierre, and the Cubs scored the go-ahead run to win the game. More bad news was on the immediate horizon, as Pujols strained his right oblique muscle the following day.

Jeff Suppan, barely visible through the Milwaukee batter, delivers a pitch. AP/WWP

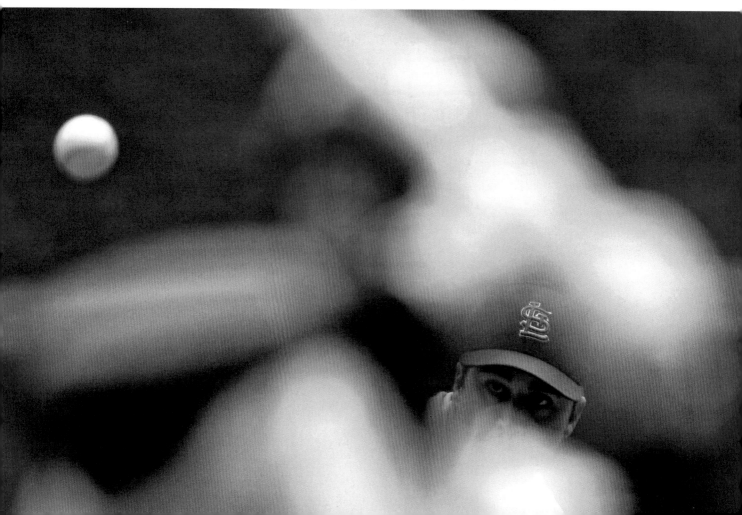

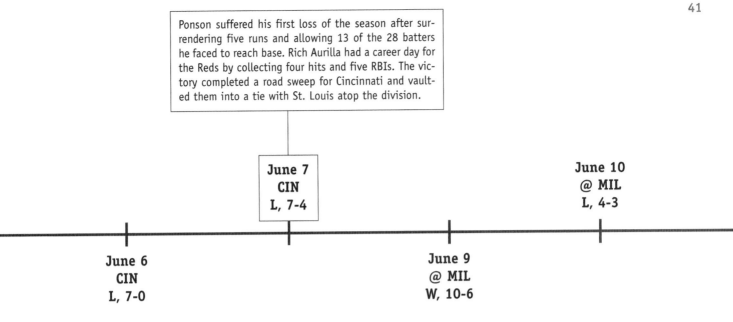

Ponson suffered his first loss of the season after surrendering five runs and allowing 13 of the 28 batters he faced to reach base. Rich Aurilla had a career day for the Reds by collecting four hits and five RBIs. The victory completed a road sweep for Cincinnati and vaulted them into a tie with St. Louis atop the division.

June 7
CIN
L, 7-4

June 10
@ MIL
L, 4-3

June 6
CIN
L, 7-0

June 9
@ MIL
W, 10-6

Chris Duncan takes out Colorado's Jamey Carroll in an attempt to break up the double play. John Grieshop/MLB Photos via Getty Images

Carpenter outdueled Oliver Perez with a masterful performance, striking out 13 batters in seven innings while surrendering just three hits and no runs. With Pujols still on the disabled list, Rolen picked up the slack by going 4-for-4 with two doubles, a run, and an RBI.

June 13
@ PIT
W, 2-1

June 15
@ PIT
W, 6-5

June 11
@ MIL
W, 7-5

June 14
@ PIT
L, 9-7

NL CENTRAL	W	L	GB
St. Louis	39	26	--
Cincinnati	37	29	2.5
Houston	35	32	5.0
Milwaukee	32	35	8.0
Chicago	26	39	13.0
Pittsburgh	26	41	14.0

RIGHT: Adam Wainwright provided the Cards bullpen with an unexpected weapon. Dilip Vishwanat/Getty Images
BELOW: David Eckstein waits for his at-bat in the dugout during the game at Comerica Park in Detroit. John Grieshop/MLB Photos via Getty Images

Missing Pujols and Eckstein, who suffered a concussion two days prior while breaking up a double play, the Cardinals received a boost from Encarnacion, who went 3-for-4 with two home runs, a double, and three RBIs. Suppan pitched 7 ⅔ innings, allowing five hits and two runs to notch his 100th career victory and sixth of the season.

June 17
COL
W, 6-5

June 20
@ CHW
L, 20-6

June 16
COL
W, 8-1

June 18
COL
W, 4-1

Scott Spiezio congratulates Juan Encarnacion after Encarnacion hit the first of two homers against the Rockies on June 17, 2006. AP/WWP

After being swept by the White Sox, the Cardinals' lead in the Central was dwindling, and the team needed a victory. They led 6-4 going into the bottom of the ninth, but Marcus Thames hit a two-run homer off Isringhausen to send the game to extra innings. In the tenth, Tyler Johnson entered the game with two outs and walked Curtis Granderson. The next batter, Placido Polanco, doubled to deep right-center to score Granderson, handing St. Louis their fifth-straight loss.

June 22
@ CHW
L, 1-0

June 24
@ DET
L, 7-6 (10)

June 21
@ CHW
L, 13-5

June 23
@ DET
L, 10-6

After being pummeled in their previous two games against the White Sox, the Cards called upon Anthony Reyes, fresh off a stint in AAA, to right the ship. The only hit the rookie allowed was a solo home run to Jim Thome in the seventh inning. The only other runner to reach base was Jermaine Dye, who ended up at third on an error by Taguchi. It would be the finest pitching performance of the regular season for St. Louis, who unfortunately could not muster any offense against Freddy Garcia and Bobby Jenks. Pujols, in his first game back from the disabled list, went 0-for-4.

Yadier Molina and Jason Marquis confer on the mound during the White Sox 13-5 thumping of the Cards on June 21, 2006. AP/WWP

Finally. The Cardinals' eight-game skid ended with a little help from the Indians' inadequate defense in the bottom of the ninth. Jhonny Peralta's throwing error allowed Eckstein to reach first base and Aaron Miles, who had tied the game earlier in the inning with a double, to score the winning run. Seat cushions—that day's giveaway at the gate—rained down from the stands as fans celebrated the victory.

June 28
CLE
W, 5-4

June 26
CLE
L, 10-3

June 25
@ DET
L, 4-1

June 27
CLE
L, 3-1

June 30
KAN
L, 7-5 (10)

NL CENTRAL	W	L	GB
St. Louis	42	34	--
Cincinnati	41	36	1.5
Milwaukee	39	39	4.0
Houston	38	40	5.0
Chicago	28	48	14.0
Pittsburgh	26	52	17.0

RIGHT: Jhonny Peralta walks off the field as the Cardinals celebrate breaking their eight-game losing streak after Peralta's error allowed the winning run to score on June 28, 2006. Fans rejoice by tossing their seat cushions, that game's giveaway, into the air. AP/WWP
BELOW: Fans were excited to see Albert Pujols back in the on-deck circle in late June after missing 15 games due to injury. Andy Altenburger/Icon SMI

JULY

JULY

The All-Star break could not have arrived soon enough for the slumping Cardinals, who over the course of June managed to squander a five-and-a-half-game lead in the Central. But a funny thing happened on the way to the All-Star game, where Albert Pujols, Scott Rolen, David Eckstein, and Chris Carpenter represented St. Louis: the Cardinals found some momentum in the form of Brad Lidge and the Houston Astros. After rallying in the top of the ninth on July 8 for two runs against Lidge, the Cardinals won the game when Pujols took Roy Oswalt deep in the tenth. The next day, they won another extra-inning affair thanks to a two-run double by Aaron Miles—again off Lidge. Coming out of the break, the reenergized Cardinals swept the Dodgers in four games, and then swept them again just one week later. But the month ended on a down note as the Cubs swept the Cards at Wrigley Field—a foreboding sign of more trouble to come.

RIGHT: Albert Pujols celebrates with his teammates after hitting a home run in the 14th to beat L.A. on July 13, 2006. Elsa/Getty Images
BELOW: Marty "The Sign Guy" Prather pays tribute to Jeff Weaver during his first start with the Cardinals. AP/WWP

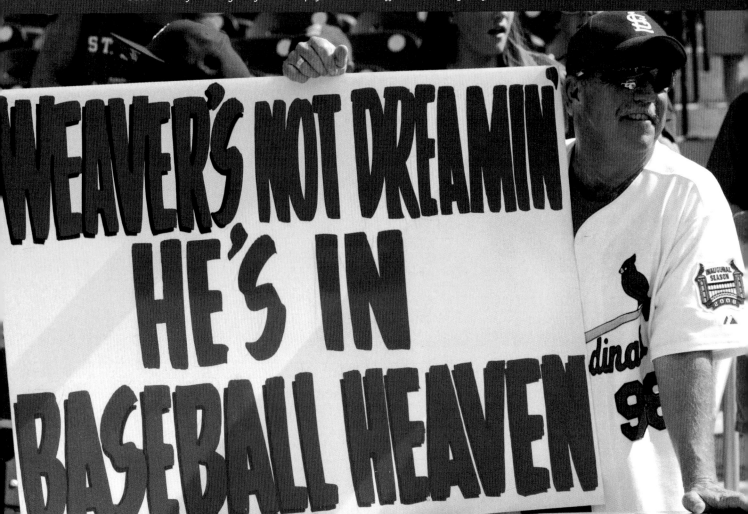

NL CENTRAL	W	L	GB
St. Louis	45	38	--
Cincinnati	44	41	2.0
Milwaukee	43	43	3.5
Houston	42	43	4.0
Chicago	31	53	14.5
Pittsburgh	29	57	17.5

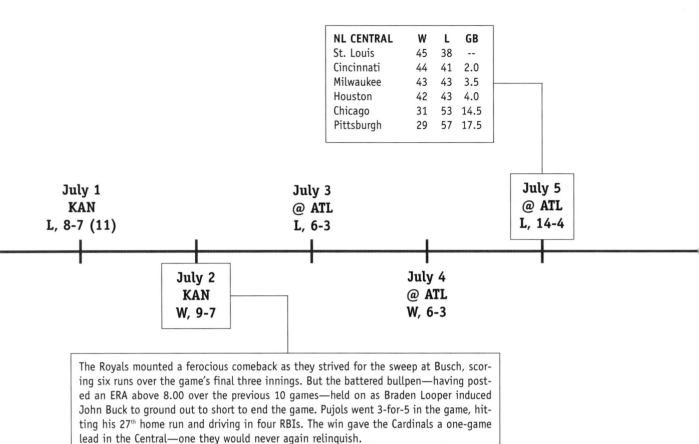

July 1
KAN
L, 8-7 (11)

July 2
KAN
W, 9-7

July 3
@ ATL
L, 6-3

July 4
@ ATL
W, 6-3

July 5
@ ATL
L, 14-4

The Royals mounted a ferocious comeback as they strived for the sweep at Busch, scoring six runs over the game's final three innings. But the battered bullpen—having posted an ERA above 8.00 over the previous 10 games—held on as Braden Looper induced John Buck to ground out to short to end the game. Pujols went 3-for-5 in the game, hitting his 27th home run and driving in four RBIs. The win gave the Cardinals a one-game lead in the Central—one they would never again relinquish.

Scott Spiezio's trademark red chin hair helped make him a fan favorite in St. Louis. John Grieshop/MLB Photos via Getty Images

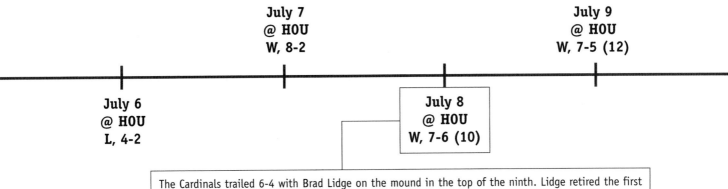

July 7
@ HOU
W, 8-2

July 9
@ HOU
W, 7-5 (12)

July 6
@ HOU
L, 4-2

July 8
@ HOU
W, 7-6 (10)

The Cardinals trailed 6-4 with Brad Lidge on the mound in the top of the ninth. Lidge retired the first two batters with ease, but Spiezio came through with a solo home run. Duncan followed with a pinch-hit single, and soon Lidge was unraveling. A walk to Eckstein moved Duncan into scoring position for Miles, who singled him home to tie the game. Roy Oswalt, in a rare relief appearance, surrendered a lead-off home run to Pujols in the tenth to put the Cards on top. Isringhausen returned to the mound in the bottom of the tenth and retired the Astros lineup in order to clinch the comeback victory. The following night, the Cards roughed up Lidge again to win their second-straight extra-inning game.

July was one of Jason Isringhausen's better months of the season. He notched four saves and posted a 0.69 ERA. Stephen Green/MLB Photos via Getty Images

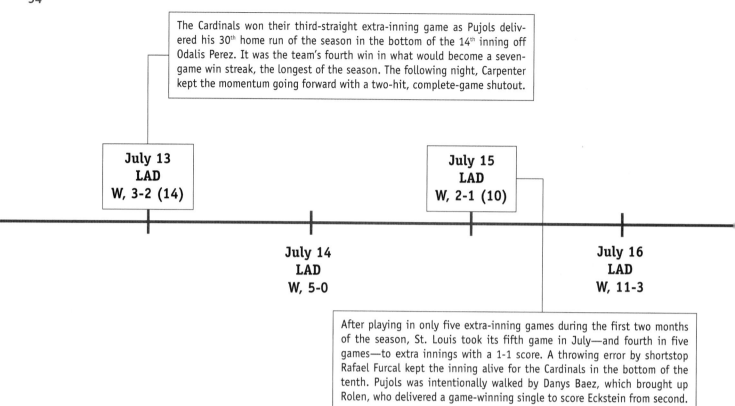

The Cardinals won their third-straight extra-inning game as Pujols delivered his 30th home run of the season in the bottom of the 14th inning off Odalis Perez. It was the team's fourth win in what would become a seven-game win streak, the longest of the season. The following night, Carpenter kept the momentum going forward with a two-hit, complete-game shutout.

July 13
LAD
W, 3-2 (14)

July 15
LAD
W, 2-1 (10)

July 14
LAD
W, 5-0

July 16
LAD
W, 11-3

After playing in only five extra-inning games during the first two months of the season, St. Louis took its fifth game in July—and fourth in five games—to extra innings with a 1-1 score. A throwing error by shortstop Rafael Furcal kept the inning alive for the Cardinals in the bottom of the tenth. Pujols was intentionally walked by Danys Baez, which brought up Rolen, who delivered a game-winning single to score Eckstein from second.

RIGHT: Albert Pujols focuses on his upcoming at-bat. AP/WWP
BELOW: Jeff Weaver was acquired from the Angels in early July to solidify the Cardinals rotation. John Sommers/Icon SMI

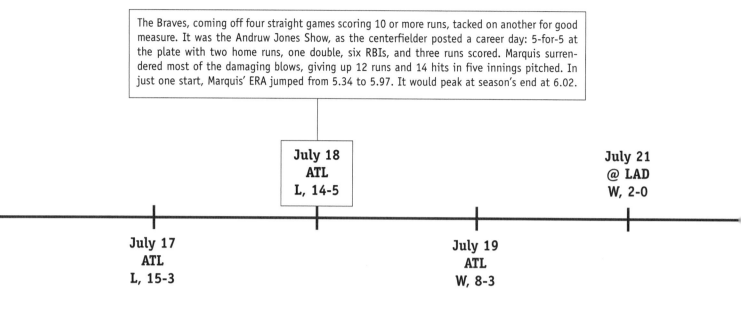

The Braves, coming off four straight games scoring 10 or more runs, tacked on another for good measure. It was the Andruw Jones Show, as the centerfielder posted a career day: 5-for-5 at the plate with two home runs, one double, six RBIs, and three runs scored. Marquis surrendered most of the damaging blows, giving up 12 runs and 14 hits in five innings pitched. In just one start, Marquis' ERA jumped from 5.34 to 5.97. It would peak at season's end at 6.02.

July 18
ATL
L, 14-5

July 21
@ LAD
W, 2-0

July 17
ATL
L, 15-3

July 19
ATL
W, 8-3

John Rodriguez waits for the pitch during a game against the Royals. Elsa/Getty Images

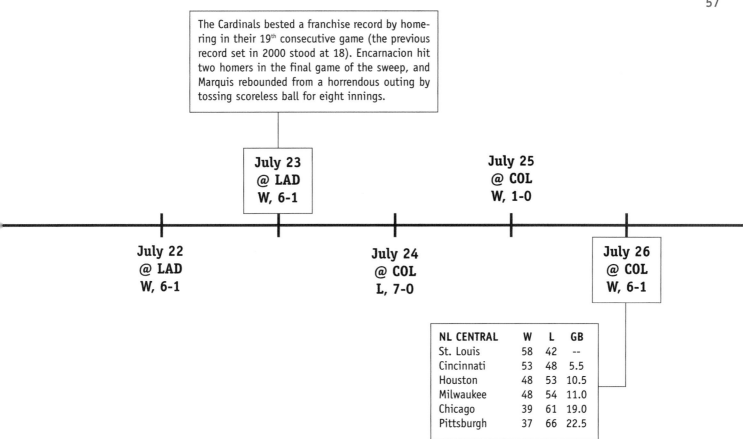

The Cardinals bested a franchise record by homering in their 19th consecutive game (the previous record set in 2000 stood at 18). Encarnacion hit two homers in the final game of the sweep, and Marquis rebounded from a horrendous outing by tossing scoreless ball for eight innings.

July 23
@ LAD
W, 6-1

July 25
@ COL
W, 1-0

July 22
@ LAD
W, 6-1

July 24
@ COL
L, 7-0

July 26
@ COL
W, 6-1

NL CENTRAL	W	L	GB
St. Louis	58	42	--
Cincinnati	53	48	5.5
Houston	48	53	10.5
Milwaukee	48	54	11.0
Chicago	39	61	19.0
Pittsburgh	37	66	22.5

Scott Rolen (No. 27) is congratulated after his game-winning single drove in David Eckstein against the Dodgers on July 15, 2006. Elsa/Getty Images

Down 4-1 in the ninth, the Cardinals mounted a rally. With Pujols on third, Edmonds on first, and two outs, Duncan stepped to the plate to face Ryan Dempster. In his first at-bat of the game after entering in a double-switch in the eighth, Duncan singled to right-center to score Pujols and move Edmonds to third. Rodriguez pinch-hit for Molina, and walked to load the bases. Dempster got out of the jam, however, as he struck out Miles to end the game. The next day, the Cubs completed the four-game sweep, their first against the Cardinals at Wrigley Field since 1972.

July 27
@ CHC
L, 5-4

July 29
@ CHC
L, 4-2

July 28
@ CHC
L, 6-5

July 30
@ CHC
L, 6-3

LEFT: So Taguchi watches helplessly as Mark Teahen's homer sails out to give the Royals the lead on July 1, 2006. AP/WWP
BELOW: Jeff Suppan turned his season around by posting a 2.39 ERA after the All-Star break. Elsa/Getty Images

AUGUST

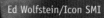
Ed Wolfstein/Icon SMI

AUGUST

Still dazed by the Cubs' crushing sweep at the end of July, St. Louis fans found that their spirits would have to suffer a bit longer as the Cardinals dropped their first four games of the month to post their second eight-game losing streak of the year. The losses were the worst kind—humiliating. In back-to-back losses to the Phillies, the Cards were first blown out despite scoring eight runs, and then manhandled by a rookie lefthander. But there was a silver lining: St. Louis didn't relinquish its hold on first place. They became the first team in Major League history to suffer two eight-game losing streaks in one season, while remaining atop the standings throughout both streaks. The rest of the NL Central wasn't posing too much competition, but then again, neither were the Cardinals, who were swept later in the month by both the Pirates and the Mets. As dreary as the month of August was, its story ended with an exclamation point in a series against Chicago, thanks to the timely hitting of backup catcher Gary Bennett. A sweep of the Cubs has a way of lifting one's spirits, indeed.

RIGHT: Albert Pujols celebrates with Yadier Molina after hitting a grand slam against the Mets on August 22, 2006. Jeff Zelevansky/Icon SMI
BELOW: Gary Bennett hangs onto the baseball after tagging out Florida's Alfredo Amezaga. AP/WWP

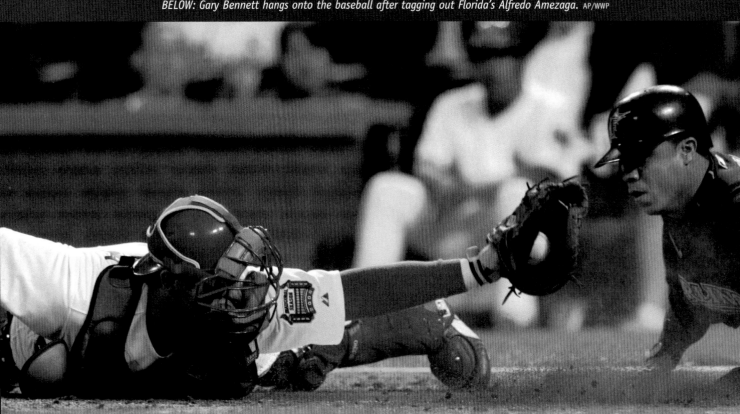

Ronnie Belliard's debut in Cardinals red began with a wimper. Despite an RBI on a sacrifice hit, Belliard went 0-for-3 with a strike-out and a throwing error. The losing skid grew to five games with the loss, and would hit eight just three days later. Ryan Howard, who was quickly becoming a contender for the NL MVP award, hit his 36th home run of the year and drove in two more runs, and St. Louis hitters were limited to just three hits over five innings by a rookie righthander who would finish the season with a 7.47 ERA.

Aug. 1
PHI
L, 5-3

Aug. 3
PHI
L, 8-1

Aug. 5
MIL
W, 4-3

Aug. 2
PHI
L, 16-8

Aug. 4
MIL
L, 4-3

NL CENTRAL	W	L	GB
St. Louis	58	50	--
Cincinnati	56	53	2.5
Milwaukee	52	57	6.5
Houston	52	57	6.5
Chicago	45	64	13.5
Pittsburgh	42	68	17.0

The team celebrates after Gary Bennett's game-winning single defeated the Cubs 2-1 on August 26, 2006. John Grieshop/MLB Photos via Getty Images

One night after Suppan had cruised through the Brewers' lineup, Weaver did the same against the Reds, striking out seven in six innings. More impressive was the St. Louis offense, which collected 17 hits—ten for extra bases—in the blowout victory. Molina had four RBIs, while Rolen and Spiezio, who pinch hit for Rolen in the eighth, combined to go 5-for-5 with a double, two home runs, and four RBIs. The 12-run spread was the largest margin of victory in the rivalry for either side since the Cardinals defeated the Reds 15-2 in 1993, thanks in no small part to Mark Whiten's four home runs and 12 RBIs.

Aug. 7
@ CIN
W, 13-1

Aug. 9
@ CIN
L, 8-7

Aug. 6
MIL
W, 7-1

Aug. 8
@ CIN
L, 10-3

A surprising slugfest erupted between two successful pitchers, Chris Carpenter and Aaron Harang, as the two starters combined to allow five home runs. However, it was the sixth one, surrendered by Isringhausen, that mattered the most. With a one-run margin in his favor in the bottom of the ninth, Isringhausen walked Rich Aurilla with one out, then gave up the game-winning home run to David Ross. It was Isringhausen's eighth blown save of the season, and his fifth loss.

Chris Duncan's performance peaked in August. He hit .361 with nine home runs in the month. AP/WWP

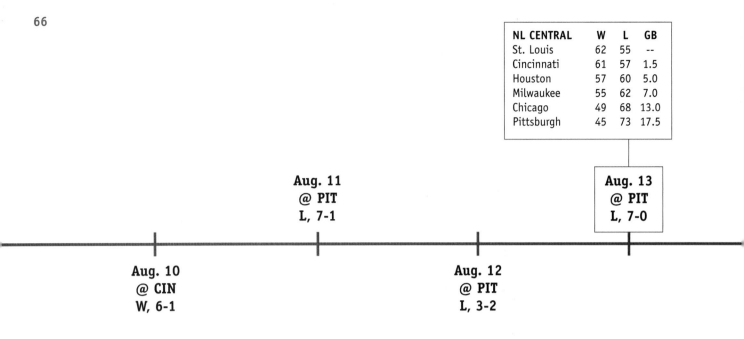

NL CENTRAL	W	L	GB
St. Louis	62	55	--
Cincinnati	61	57	1.5
Houston	57	60	5.0
Milwaukee	55	62	7.0
Chicago	49	68	13.0
Pittsburgh	45	73	17.5

Aug. 11
@ PIT
L, 7-1

Aug. 13
@ PIT
L, 7-0

Aug. 10
@ CIN
W, 6-1

Aug. 12
@ PIT
L, 3-2

RIGHT: Braden Looper posted a 3.12 ERA and 5-2 record for the Cardinals after the All-Star break. Anthony J. Causi/Icon SMI
BELOW: Preston Wilson was signed on August 19 by the Cardinals, and hit eight home runs down the stretch. John Grieshop/MLB Photos via Getty Images

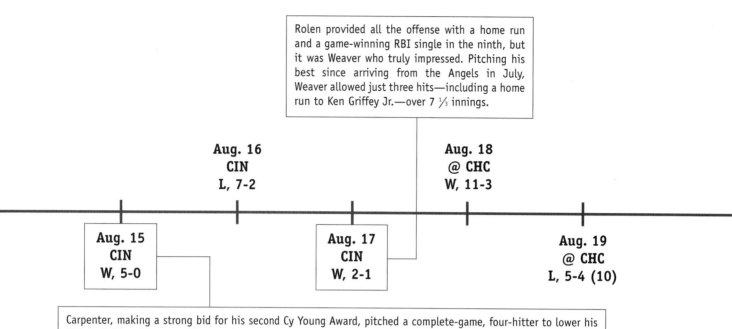

Rolen provided all the offense with a home run and a game-winning RBI single in the ninth, but it was Weaver who truly impressed. Pitching his best since arriving from the Angels in July, Weaver allowed just three hits—including a home run to Ken Griffey Jr.—over 7 ⅓ innings.

Aug. 16
CIN
L, 7-2

Aug. 18
@ CHC
W, 11-3

Aug. 15
CIN
W, 5-0

Aug. 17
CIN
W, 2-1

Aug. 19
@ CHC
L, 5-4 (10)

Carpenter, making a strong bid for his second Cy Young Award, pitched a complete-game, four-hitter to lower his ERA to 3.09 and improve his record to 11-6. Duncan went 3-for-5 with a two-run home run, while Belliard went 3-for-3 with a pair of RBIs. More importantly, with their lead just a game and a half over the Reds, the Cardinals needed a bit of breathing room in a key home series against Cincinnati. They got it with their ace on the mound.

Jim Edmonds scores on a close play at the plate in the ninth inning against the Cubs on August 19, 2006. Ron Vesely/MLB Photos via Getty Images

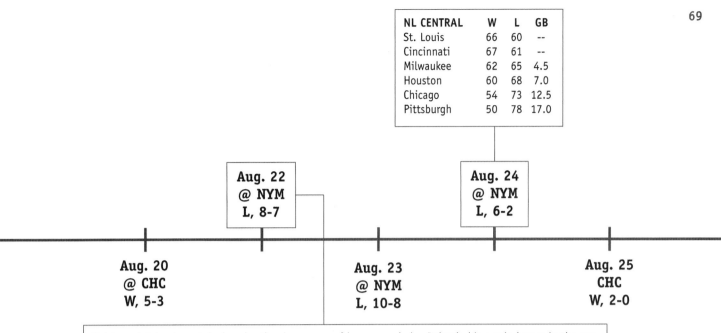

NL CENTRAL	W	L	GB
St. Louis	66	60	--
Cincinnati	67	61	--
Milwaukee	62	65	4.5
Houston	60	68	7.0
Chicago	54	73	12.5
Pittsburgh	50	78	17.0

Aug. 22
@ NYM
L, 8-7

Aug. 24
@ NYM
L, 6-2

Aug. 20
@ CHC
W, 5-3

Aug. 23
@ NYM
L, 10-8

Aug. 25
CHC
W, 2-0

Pujols and Delgado matched each other in a game of home-run derby. Delgado hit a solo homer in the second, and Pujols answered with a three-run shot in the fourth. Then in the top of the fifth, Pujols hit a grand slam, to which Delgado responded with a grand slam of his own to make it 7-5. The Mets tacked on another run in the sixth, then Beltran took care of the rest with a walk-off, two-run homer off Isringhausen.

Albert Pujols sports the throwback uniform of the Negro League St. Louis Stars in an August game against Pittsburgh. AP/WWP

One night after hitting a game-winning, walk-off single, Gary Bennett rose to the occasion again. After the Cubs battled back to tie the game at six, the Cards entered the bottom of the ninth hoping for the sweep. Pujols singled to start the inning, and after a ground out, an infield single, and a walk the bases were loaded with one out. Bob Howry got Miles to hit a grounder to shortstop Ronny Cedeno, who threw home to get the force out on Pujols. With two outs, Bennett hammered a 1-0 pitch over the left field wall for a walk-off grand slam. The sweep increased St. Louis' lead over Cincinnati to three games.

Aug. 27
CHC
W, 10-6

Aug. 30
FLA
W, 13-6

Aug. 26
CHC
W, 2-1

Aug. 29
FLA
L, 9-1

Aug. 31
FLA
W, 5-2

Cardinals hitters pounded out a season-best 20 hits to snap Florida's nine-game win streak. The heart of the St. Louis order—Pujols, Rolen, Encarnacion, and Wilson—combined for five doubles, one home run, four singles, eight RBIs, and seven runs scored.

LEFT: Albert Pujols hugs Gary Bennett after Bennett connected for a walk-off grand slam against the Cubs on August 27, 2006. AP/WWP
BELOW: Gary Bennett (No. 28) became quite the surprise hero for the Cardinals in late August. AP/WWP

SEPTEMBER

Although expected to three-peat as NL Central champions, the 2006 Cardinals had encountered their fair share of troubles: two eight-game losing streaks, numerous injuries, and 10 sweeps at the hands of their opponents. Still, the team liked its chances heading into September as they sported a five-game lead over a .500 Cincinnati ball club. But it was Houston—not Cincinnati—who would give the Cards a run for their money. St. Louis' freefall gained momentum mid-month, when Isringhausen opted for season-ending surgery, leaving a young bullpen in disarray. By month's end, St. Louis found itself staring down its third eight-game losing streak of the season. This time, the skid *would* cost them their divisional lead—and possibly a slot in the playoffs. The Cards were on the verge of a monumental collapse, and not even Carpenter could keep them from tailspinning out of control. Luckily for the Redbirds, they still had the reigning MVP in Pujols, who provided the parachute with a three-run homer off Cla Meredith on September 27, which stopped the losing streak at seven games. Hope began to well as the season's final series, at home against Milwaukee, would raise all the stakes. October baseball hung in the balance.

Tony La Russa congratulates Chris Carpenter after his complete-game shutout against the Astros on September 11, 2006. Elsa/Getty Images

BELOW: At times, watching the Cardinals in Setpember was hard on one's nerves—especially for the players themselves. AP/WWP

Prior to the game, Pujols participated in the Cardinals' annual "buddy walk" to focus attention on those with Down Syndrome. More than a few children with Down Syndrome in attendance asked him to hit a home run in the game. Pujols obliged, homering in each of his first three at-bats to notch five RBIs as St. Louis won with ease, 6-3. Reyes pitched 6 ⅓ scoreless innings, allowing just four hits while striking out nine.

Sept. 1
PIT
W, 3-1

Sept. 3
PIT
W, 6-3

Sept. 5
@ WAS
W, 2-0

Sept. 2
PIT
L, 1-0

Sept. 4
@ WAS
L, 4-1

Suppan worked 7 ⅔ scoreless innings to continue his dominant second half of the season. Pujols hit a solo home run—his 44th of the year—and Isringhausen picked up his 33rd save of the year. It would be Izzy's last, however, as the veteran closer finally succumbed to an injured hip that had bothered him for a bulk of the season. Two weeks later, he would decide to undergo season-ending surgery.

When his team needed him most in the month of September, Albert Pujols delivered with a .368 average and 27 RBIs. Dilip Vishwanat/Getty Images

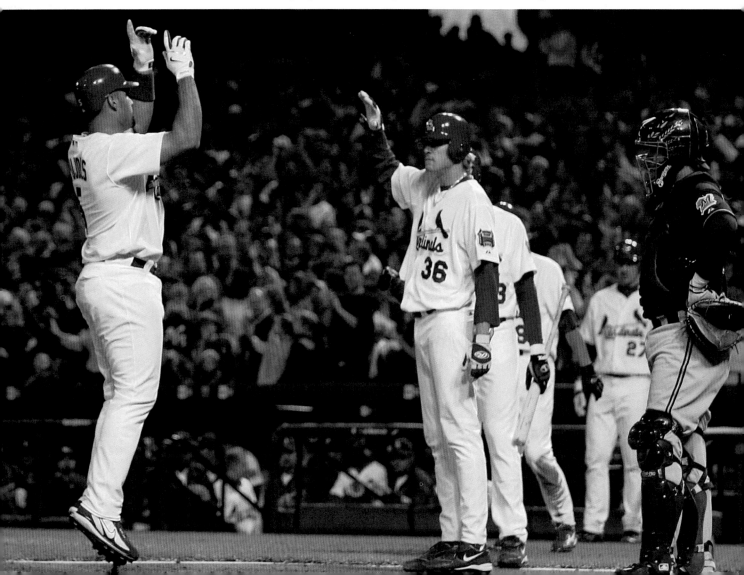

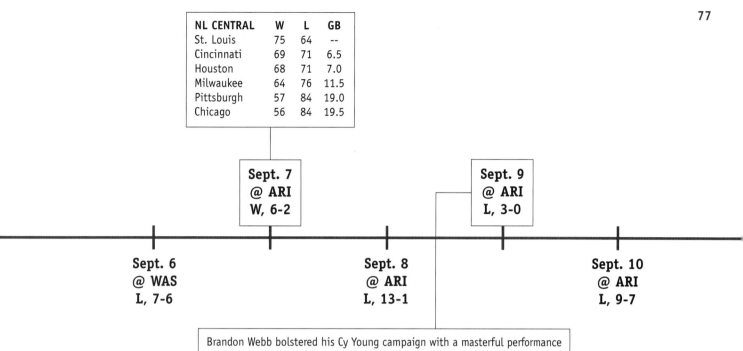

NL CENTRAL	W	L	GB
St. Louis	75	64	--
Cincinnati	69	71	6.5
Houston	68	71	7.0
Milwaukee	64	76	11.5
Pittsburgh	57	84	19.0
Chicago	56	84	19.5

Sept. 7
@ ARI
W, 6-2

Sept. 9
@ ARI
L, 3-0

Sept. 6
@ WAS
L, 7-6

Sept. 8
@ ARI
L, 13-1

Sept. 10
@ ARI
L, 9-7

Brandon Webb bolstered his Cy Young campaign with a masterful performance against the Cardinals. Relying almost entirely on his fastball, Webb allowed just one base hit, a double to Rolen, en route to a complete-game shutout.

Scott Rolen lunges to tag Pittsburgh's Ryan Doumit at third base. Dilip Vishwanat/Getty Images

Carpenter improved his ERA at new Busch Stadium to a miniscule 1.47 with a six-hit, complete game shutout. It was his fifth complete game and third shutout of the season, with each of the shutouts coming at Busch. His overall ERA stood at 2.84, his lowest mark since late July.

Duncan homered twice, giving him 15 home runs after the All-Star break—one short of the Cardinal rookie record of 16, set by Pujols in 2001. Despite going 2-for-4 with three runs and four RBIs, Duncan was upstaged by Rolen, who also hit two homers but went 3-for-4 with a double and seven RBIs. The following day, Cardinals batters spoiled Matt Morris' return to St. Louis by ambushing him for four runs in the first inning.

Sept. 11
HOU
W, 7-0

Sept. 13
HOU
L, 5-1

Sept. 16
SFO
6-1

Sept. 12
HOU
W, 6-5

Sept. 15
SFO
W, 14-4

Pujols got the best of Brad Lidge yet again with a two-out, two-run double to deep left, which gave the Cardinals a 5-4 victory and a seven-game lead over the Astros. In the ninth, Lidge allowed a lead-off single to Rodriguez, who was removed for pinchrunner Skip Schumaker. After Jose Vizcaino sacrificed Schumaker to second, Lidge retired Wilson on a strikeout and plunked Spiezio, putting the winning run on first. Pujols then drove a two-strike pitch down the left-field line to give the Cardinals the win.

RIGHT: Cardinals fans grew to like Ronnie Belliard—and his tongue—as the regular season came to a close. Dilip Vishwanat/Getty Images
BELOW: Cardinals players—including Jeff Weaver—had plenty to ponder as their divisional lead grew smaller by the day. AP/WWP

80

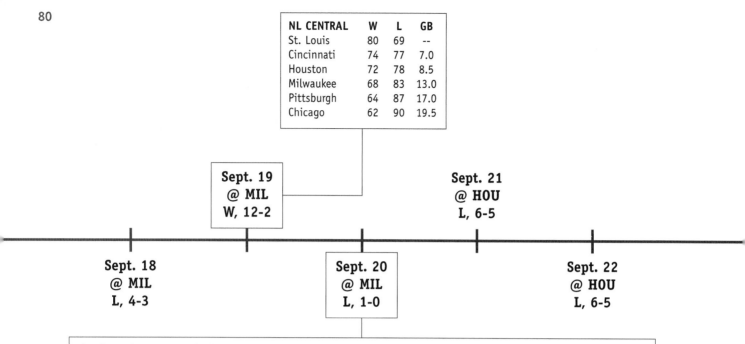

NL CENTRAL	W	L	GB
St. Louis	80	69	--
Cincinnati	74	77	7.0
Houston	72	78	8.5
Milwaukee	68	83	13.0
Pittsburgh	64	87	17.0
Chicago	62	90	19.5

Sept. 19
@ MIL
W, 12-2

Sept. 21
@ HOU
L, 6-5

Sept. 18
@ MIL
L, 4-3

Sept. 20
@ MIL
L, 1-0

Sept. 22
@ HOU
L, 6-5

The first of seven straight losses seemed inconspicuous on the surface. Suppan and Brewers rookie Carlos Villanueva squared off in a seven-inning pitcher's duel, each holding the other team scoreless. But in the bottom of the ninth, St. Louis turned to lefty Tyler Johnson to face Geoff Jenkins, who hit a solo walk-off home run to end the stalemate. With Isringhausen on the shelf for the rest of the season, Tony La Russa was forced to find new roles for his relievers. The next six games—all losses—would give La Russa and his coaching staff plenty to discuss as far as the pen was concerned.

Preston Wilson was one of a few Cardinals hoping to make the playoffs for the first time. Elsa/Getty Images

With their lead down to just five and a half games over the Reds and Astros, St. Louis needed to win its final two games against Houston to check the upstart Astros. After battling back in the top of the ninth to score two runs and take a 5-4 lead, St. Louis appeared well on its way to taking its first game of the series. Johnson was called upon in the bottom of the ninth with Houston's best two left-handed batters—Lance Berkman and Luke Scott—due up. Johnson walked Morgan Ensberg on four pitches to start the frame, then allowed Berkman to reach on a bloop single to center. Scott promptly pounded a pitch over the right-field wall for a three-run homer to give the Astros the victory.

NL CENTRAL	W	L	GB
St. Louis	80	76	--
Houston	79	78	1.5
Cincinnati	78	79	2.5
Milwaukee	73	84	7.5
Pittsburgh	65	92	15.5
Chicago	64	94	17.0

Sept. 23
@ HOU
L, 7-4

Sept. 25
SDG
L, 6-5

Sept. 27
SDG
W, 4-2

Sept. 24
@ HOU
L, 7-3

Sept. 26
SDG
L, 7-5

With the national media ready to write the Cardinals' obituary, St. Louis looked to its MVP, Albert Pujols, for support. In the eighth inning Pujols delivered a three-run homer off submariner Cla Meredith to give the Cardinals a 4-2 lead. This time, the bullpen did its job. In a telling move, La Russa went to Adam Wainwright to get the final three outs. The rookie struck out the first two batters he faced, then quickly worked around a two-out double to finish off the Padres and earn his second career save. Later that night, Houston won a 15-inning game against the Pirates to keep the pressure on the Cardinals.

Fans at Busch Stadium applaud Scott Spiezio after he hit a three-run triple against the Brewers on September 30, 2006. Dilip Vishwanat/Getty Images

NL CENTRAL	W	L	GB
St. Louis	83	78	--
Houston	82	80	1.5
Cincinnati	80	82	3.5
Milwaukee	75	87	8.5
Pittsburgh	67	95	16.5
Chicago	66	96	17.5

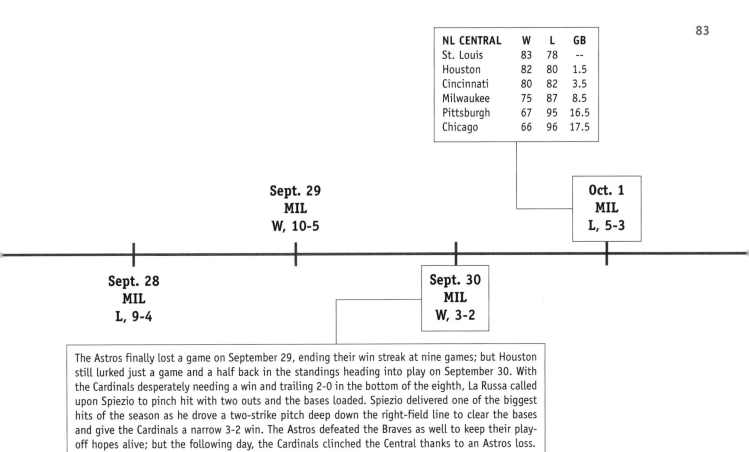

Sept. 29
MIL
W, 10-5

Oct. 1
MIL
L, 5-3

Sept. 28
MIL
L, 9-4

Sept. 30
MIL
W, 3-2

The Astros finally lost a game on September 29, ending their win streak at nine games; but Houston still lurked just a game and a half back in the standings heading into play on September 30. With the Cardinals desperately needing a win and trailing 2-0 in the bottom of the eighth, La Russa called upon Spiezio to pinch hit with two outs and the bases loaded. Spiezio delivered one of the biggest hits of the season as he drove a two-strike pitch deep down the right-field line to clear the bases and give the Cardinals a narrow 3-2 win. The Astros defeated the Braves as well to keep their playoff hopes alive; but the following day, the Cardinals clinched the Central thanks to an Astros loss.

LEFT: Scott Rolen receives a champagne shower after the Cardinals clinched the NL Central on the last day of the season. AP/WWP
BELOW: Albert Pujols douses Gary Bennett with beer during the Cardinals' celebration of their third-straight divisional title. AP/WWP

NLDS

Respect. The Cardinals weren't given much of it entering the NLDS by sportswriters who had watched them "back their way into the postseason." St. Louis finished the regular season by going 4-9 after playing mediocre baseball for weeks. San Diego, meanwhile, had spent the entire season in a dogfight in the competitive NL West; had beaten the Cardinals in four of six games in 2006; and finished the regular season on a 10-4 run to clinch their division. They featured one of baseball's strongest pitching staffs and a balanced offensive attack, so it was easy to see why so many baseball pundits picked the Padres to advance. But for the Cardinals, the postseason wiped the slate clean. The near collapse, the losing streaks, the inconsistent play: all of that was now a thing of the past. La Russa breathed new life into the team, encouraging his players to savor the moment. Meanwhile, many fans just hoped that the Cardinals wouldn't embarrass themselves. Few were ready for what St. Louis had in store.

BELOW: Preston Wilson and Gary Bennett relax on the outfield grass during batting practice prior to Game 2 of the NLDS. AP/WWP

After cruising through the first three innings, San Diego starter Jake Peavy surrendered a lead-off single to Duncan in the fourth. Pujols fouled a pop-up back to the screen that Mike Piazza failed to catch and, on the eighth pitch of his at-bat, homered to left-center field to plate the first two runs of the game. An Edmonds single, a Rolen double, and a sacrifice fly from Encarnacion gave the Cardinals their third run of the inning.

Dave Roberts tripled off Carpenter with one out for his third hit of the game. Brian Giles followed with a sacrifice fly for the Padres' lone run of the game. Carpenter, who allowed just one run and struck out seven, would exit the game the following inning after allowing a triple and a walk.

**Oct. 3
Game 1
@ SDG
W, 5-1**

**Top 4th
STL 3
SDG 0**

**Bot 6th
STL 5
SDG 1**

**Top 6th
STL 5
SDG 0**

**Bot 9th
STL 5
SDG 1**

Molina's RBI single to score Belliard knocked Peavy out of the game. The Padres hurler surrendered 11 hits in 5 ⅓ innings.

In his first postseason appearance, Wainwright struck out Russell Branyan and Mike Cameron swinging, then closed the door on Game 1 by inducing Ryan Klesko to fly out to left.

Adam Wainwright made his postseason debut in the shadows of Petco Park. John R. McCutchen/San Diego Union-Tribune via Getty Images

Wilson doubled off David Wells to lead off the inning. With no outs, the Padres chose to pitch to Pujols, who smacked a two-strike pitch to left field to score Wilson. Pujols advanced to second on the throw home, and two batters later stood at third with two outs. Edmonds came through with an RBI single, and that would be all the offense the Cardinals would need.

The Padres' best scoring opportunity came with two outs in the eighth, as Josh Barfield doubled on the second pitch he saw from Wainwright. But Wainwright got Adrian Gonzalez to ground out to end the inning. Prior to Wainwright, Cardinals relievers Johnson, Flores, and Josh Kinney did an exceptional job, allowing just two baserunners while striking out four of the 10 batters they faced.

Top 4th
STL 2
SDG 0

Bot 8th
STL 2
SDG 0

Oct. 5
Game 2
@ SDG
W, 2-0

Bot 5th
STL 2
SDG 0

Bot 9th
STL 2
SDG 0

Weaver's 79th pitch of the day struck out Roberts swinging. Weaver surrendered just two hits and three walks in five innings, and retired 12 of the final 13 batters he faced.

Wainwright slammed the door shut for the second game in a row by punching out Cameron and Branyan, and getting Josh Bard to ground out.

LEFT: David Eckstein lays down a squeeze bunt in Game 4 of the NLDS. Stephen Dunn/Getty Images
BELOW: Yadier Molina congratulates Albert Pujols after the Cardinals won Game 2 of the NLDS. Stephen Dunn/Getty Images

Suppan pitched around a first-and-third, nobody-out situation. With Roberts on third and Todd Walker at first, Suppan induced Giles to weakly ground out. Roberts was then thrown out at home on a Piazza ground ball to first, and Molina ended the inning by picking off Piazza at first.

Facing the heart of the Cardinals order after his team put three runs on the board, Chris Young struck out Pujols, Edmonds, and Rolen—each of them swinging for strike three. Young recorded nine strikeouts in 6 ⅔ innings pitched.

Top 1ˢᵗ
STL 0
SDG 0

Bot 4ᵗʰ
SDG 3
STL 0

**Oct. 7
Game 3
SDG
L, 3-1**

Top 4ᵗʰ
SDG 3
STL 0

Bot 8ᵗʰ
SDG 3
STL 1

With runners on first and second, Branyan tripled to right to score both runners. Geoff Blum knocked in Branyan with a sacrifice fly to give the Padres a three-run cushion.

The Cardinals only run came in the eighth as pinch hitter So Taguchi homered against reliever Scott Linebrink. Taguchi had only hit two home runs in 316 at-bats during the regular season.

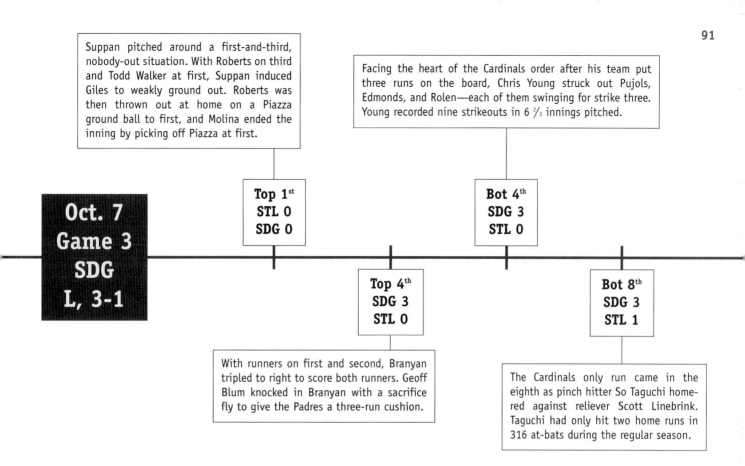

LEFT: Tony La Russa did some of his finest managing in the 2006 playoffs. AP/WWP
BELOW: Yadier Molina tags out Dave Roberts at home during the first inning of Game 3 of the NLDS. Christian Petersen/Getty Images

San Diego wasted no time in Game 4, loading the bases with one out in the first. In uncharacteristic fashion, Carpenter walked in a run, his second walk in a row. The next batter, Cameron, hit into a fielder's choice to score another run as the Cardinals nabbed the out at second. Carpenter then walked Blum—his third walk of the inning—to again load the bases before retiring Barfield to end the inning.

The Cards put Game 4 in the bag with a four-run sixth. Pujols scored on Encarnacion's one-out triple. San Diego went to its bullpen, and the offensive flood gates opened for St. Louis. Reliever Cla Meredith entered the game and nailed Belliard with a pitch. Two singles, a throwing error, and a squeeze bunt later, the Cardinals had tacked on three more runs.

Top 1st
SDG 2
STL 0

Bot 6th
STL 6
SDG 2

Oct. 8
Game 4
SDG
W, 6-2

Bot 1st
STL 2
SDG 2

Top 9th
STL 6
SDG 2

The Cardinals rallied in the bottom half of the first against former teammate Woody Williams. After Edmonds was hit by a pitch and Encarnacion walked to load the bases, Belliard hit a bases-loaded, two-run single to tie the game.

Wainwright began the ninth by striking out Cameron for the third time in the series. But Klesko drilled a double to deep center, and Barfield followed with a single to put runners on the corners with one out. Wainwright struck out Khalil Greene for the second out, and sent the Cardinals on to the NLCS by getting Roberts to ground out to Pujols.

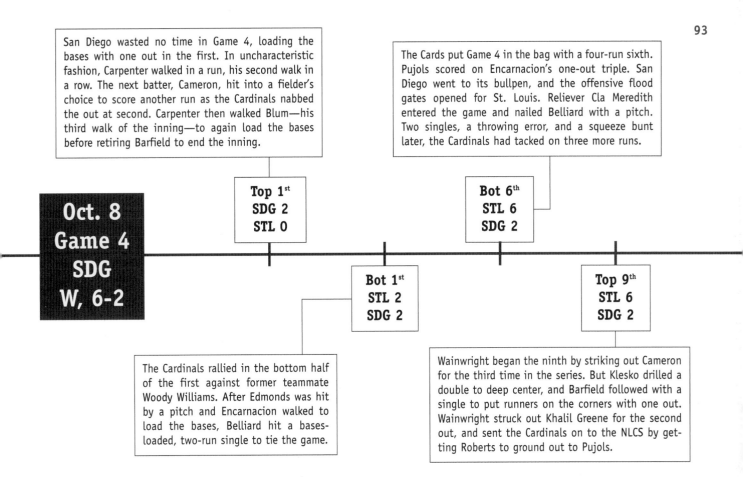

LEFT: Players celebrate on the field after advancing to the NLCS to face the Mets. Christian Petersen/Getty Images
BELOW: Players rush onto the field after the last out of the NLDS. AP/WWP

NLCS

The same critics who picked the Cardinals to lose to the Padres also granted the NLCS to the Mets. The Mets offense—featuring Carlos Delgado, David Wright, Jose Reyes, and proclaimed "Cardinal killer" Carlos Beltran—was deemed too talented for Cardinals pitchers to contain. Despite the loss of Orlando Hernandez and Pedro Martinez to injury, New York still had Tom Glavine—with his 33 career postseason starts—ready to pitch in two games of the series. They also boasted the league's best bullpen—anchored by left-handed flamethrower Billy Wagner—in case the team's lesser starters faltered. And they were, of course, the Mets, the lone surviving New York ball club—reason enough for baseball enthusiasts who had missed the arrival of the Mets bandwagon in May to climb aboard in October. Plenty of seats were still available on the St. Louis bandwagon as it pulled up to Shea Stadium on a soggy October 11. Passengers would have plenty of time to board: approximately nine days, all the way up to the moment Adam Wainwright unleashed the prettiest curve ball you ever did see for a called strike three.

Preston Wilson and Juan Encarnacion share a laugh while Albert Pujols gestures prior to Game 1 of the NLCS. Jim McIsaac/Getty Images

Molina and Weaver both singled to the opposite field with one out to give St. Louis its best scoring chance of the night. With a 2-0 count in his favor, Eckstein hit a sharp line drive to David Wright, who caught it and quickly doubled Molina off second to end the inning.

Weaver didn't make many mistakes on the mound—until he faced Carlos Beltran in the sixth. With two outs and Lo Duca on first after a single, Weaver let a 2-2 pitch get too much of the plate, and Beltran turned on it to smack a two-run homer to right field. That was all the offense the Mets would need to take Game 1.

Top 3rd
STL 0
NYM 0

Bot 6th
NYM 2
STL 0

Oct. 12 Game 1 @ NYM L, 2-0

Top 6th
STL 0
NYM 0

Tom Glavine brought his A-game in Game 1. In the sixth, he surrendered a one-out single to Wilson, but got Pujols to line out to the shortstop on a hard-hit ball and Encarnacion to fly out to right. On the night, Glavine sent the Cards down in order in four of his seven innings pitched.

Cardinals pitchers will not miss facing Carlos Beltran and Carlos Delgado. Chris McGrath/Getty Images

The Mets wasted no time in pouncing on Carpenter in the first, as Jose Reyes doubled, Beltran walked, and Carlos Delgado deposited a home run over the centerfield wall. Carpenter allowed another tally in the second, but then regrouped to post two relatively uneventful innings.

The Cardinals tied it up on a two-run home run by Edmonds after a Pujols walk. It was Edmonds' fourth career NLCS home run, and his eighth overall playoff homer.

**Oct. 13
Game 2
@ NYM
W, 9-6**

**Bot 1ˢᵗ
NYM 3
STL 0**

**Top 3ʳᵈ
STL 4
NYM 4**

**Top 2ⁿᵈ
NYM 3
STL 2**

The Cardinals fought back in the second to load the bases with nobody out against John Maine. Belliard popped out for the first out, but then Molina doubled to score two runs. Maine averted further damage by striking out Carpenter and getting Eckstein to line out to end the inning.

So Taguchi rounds the bases after homering against Billy Wagner in Game 2 of the NLCS. Rich Pilling/MLB Photos via Getty Images

With Guillermo Mota on the mound, St. Louis mounted a two-out rally to tie the game. Pujols singled, Edmonds walked, and then Spiezio delivered his second memorable triple of the season. This one came on an 0-2 pitch and was nearly robbed at the wall by Shawn Green. Both Edmonds and Pujols scored on the hit, but Spiezio was later stranded at third.

Tyler Johnson entered the game with the sole purpose of retiring Delgado, who had already homered twice in the game. After Johnson struck him out, Wainwright recorded the final two outs of the game to even the series at one game apiece.

Top 7th
STL 6
NYM 6

Bot 9th
STL 9
NYM 6

Bot 5th
NYM 5
STL 4

Top 9th
STL 9
NYM 6

Delgado got the best of Carpenter again with an opposite-field home run to give the Mets a one-run lead. Only one other time during the '06 season did Carpenter allow two home runs in the same game to the same batter (Lance Berkman).

Billy Wagner took the mound to face Taguchi, who worked a full count into an eight-pitch at-bat and then homered to give the Cards the lead. Wagner then surrendered a double to Pujols, who scored two batters later on a Spiezio double. Encarnacion singled in Spiezio to increase the lead to three.

Scott Rolen did not enjoy his time on the bench in Game 2 of the NLCS. Rich Pilling/MLB Photos via Getty Images

Eckstein singled to open the bottom of the first, but was picked off for the first out. Steve Trachsel got himself back into hot water by walking Wilson and surrendering a single to Pujols. With two outs, Spiezio tripled to right to score both runners. Trachsel walked the next two batters, but then struck out Molina to end the inning.

After allowing the minimum number of baserunners in four straight innings, Suppan walked Shawn Green to start the eighth. But New York would do no damage, as Suppan pitched around the walk to complete his sensational start. He allowed just three hits and one walk on the night. Only two Mets batters reached scoring position, and both were stranded.

Bot 1ˢᵗ
STL 2
NYM 0

Top 8ᵗʰ
STL 5
NYM 0

Oct. 14
Game 3
NYM
W, 5-0

Bot 2ⁿᵈ
STL 5
NYM 0

Suppan picked a great time to hit his second career home run to lead off the inning. Trachsel was relieved in the middle of the inning by Darren Oliver, whose third pitch of the night was a wild one, allowing another run to score. Edmonds drove in the game's final run on a ground out to first.

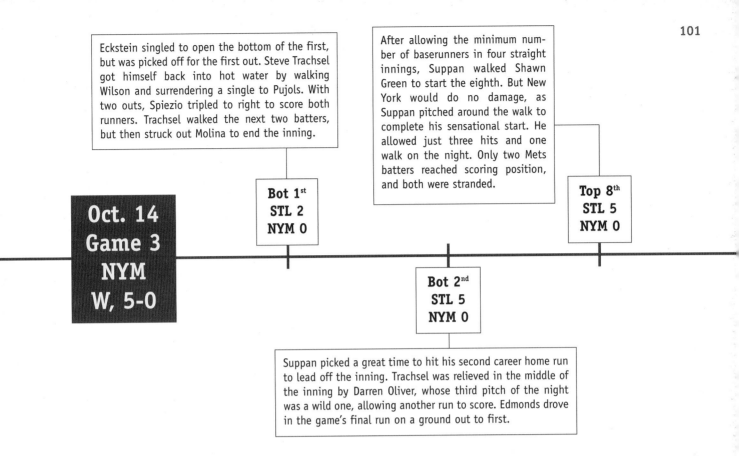

LEFT: A fan holds up a creative sign during Game 3 of the NLCS. Elsa/Getty Images
BELOW: Jeff Suppan logged his first of two impressive starts against the Mets in Game 3 of the NLCS. Dilip Vishwanat/Getty Images

After his teammates gave him a 1-0 lead in the bottom of the second, Anthony Reyes surrendered solo home runs to Beltran and Wright. The Cardinals would come back in the bottom of the inning to tie the game on an Encarnacion triple.

The Cardinals pen finally cracked in a big way for the first time in the '06 postseason. Josh Hancock allowed two runs and four baserunners without getting a single out, and Johnson could not stop the bleeding. Another single and a double plated four more runs for New York, who quickly turned a slim two-run margin into a rout. The Cardinals would go on to get solo home runs from Edmonds and Molina, but Game 4 was all about the Mets' mighty offense flexing its muscles.

Top 3rd
NYM 2
STL 1

Top 6th
NYM 11
STL 3

Oct. 15
Game 4
NYM
L, 12-5

Top 5th
NYM 5
STL 2

In the top of the fifth, Brad Thompson relieved Reyes, who had thrown 86 pitches through four innings. Thompson quickly found himself in trouble after a Belliard error and a single placed runners on first and second with no one out. Delgado made the Cardinals pay with his third home run of the series, a three-run shot.

Jim Edmonds makes a spectacular catch on a ball hit by Jose Reyes in the sixth inning of Game 4 of the NLCS. Elsa/Getty Images

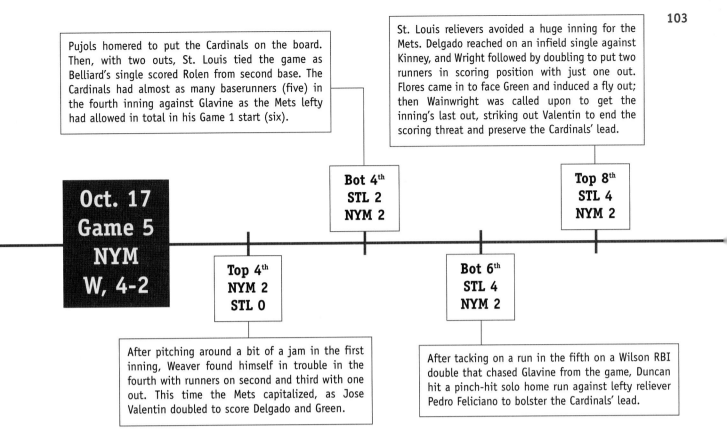

Pujols homered to put the Cardinals on the board. Then, with two outs, St. Louis tied the game as Belliard's single scored Rolen from second base. The Cardinals had almost as many baserunners (five) in the fourth inning against Glavine as the Mets lefty had allowed in total in his Game 1 start (six).

St. Louis relievers avoided a huge inning for the Mets. Delgado reached on an infield single against Kinney, and Wright followed by doubling to put two runners in scoring position with just one out. Flores came in to face Green and induced a fly out; then Wainwright was called upon to get the inning's last out, striking out Valentin to end the scoring threat and preserve the Cardinals' lead.

Bot 4th
STL 2
NYM 2

Top 8th
STL 4
NYM 2

Oct. 17
Game 5
NYM
W, 4-2

Top 4th
NYM 2
STL 0

Bot 6th
STL 4
NYM 2

After pitching around a bit of a jam in the first inning, Weaver found himself in trouble in the fourth with runners on second and third with one out. This time the Mets capitalized, as Jose Valentin doubled to score Delgado and Green.

After tacking on a run in the fifth on a Wilson RBI double that chased Glavine from the game, Duncan hit a pinch-hit solo home run against lefty reliever Pedro Feliciano to bolster the Cardinals' lead.

Jeff Weaver pumps his fist during Game 5 of the NLCS. Jamie Squire/Getty Images

Reyes set the tone for Game 6 in his first at-bat by homering off Carpenter. The blow was especially significant because the Cardinals had failed to take advantage of a bases-loaded scoring chance in the top of the first.

The Cardinals got after Wagner for the second time in the NLCS after Encarnacion singled and Rolen doubled to place two runners in scoring position with no outs. Taguchi would rip a pinch-hit double two batters later to score both runners, but that was all the Cardinals would get, as Wagner got Eckstein to ground out to end the game.

Oct. 18
Game 6
@ NYM
L, 4-2

Bot 1st
NYM 1
STL 0

Top 9th
NYM 4
STL 2

Bot 7th
NYM 4
STL 0

To start the seventh, Looper relieved Carpenter, who was lifted for a pinch-hitter in the sixth inning despite having thrown just 76 pitches. A pair of singles and a pair of stolen bases put runners on second and third with two outs for Lo Duca, who singled to center to double the Mets' lead.

Lefthander Tyler Johnson was one of many Cardinals pitchers to rise to the occasion in the 2006 playoffs. Jim McIsaac/Getty Images

Suppan recorded the first two outs of the game before Beltran doubled and Delgado walked. Wright followed with a single to score Beltran and give the Mets the early lead.

With Suppan pitching well, the Cardinals looked to build a lead in the fifth. Belliard singled to lead off the inning and was sacrificed to second by Suppan. Eckstein was then hit by a pitch to put two runners on with one out. But Wilson struck out swinging, and Oliver Perez got out of the inning when Pujols popped out to the shortstop.

**Oct. 19
Game 7
@ NYM
W, 3-1**

**Bot 1ˢᵗ
NYM 1
STL 0**

**Top 5ᵗʰ
STL 1
NYM 1**

**Top 2ⁿᵈ
STL 1
NYM 1**

The Cardinals immediately fought back in the second, as Edmonds opened the inning with a single. Molina singled two batters later to move Edmonds to third, and Edmonds then scored on a sacrifice by Belliard.

Yadier Molina watches his home run take flight in Game 7 of the NLCS. AP/WWP

The game's momentum shifted dramatically heading into the sixth after Endy Chavez made a spectacular catch at the left-field wall to rob Rolen of a home run. But Suppan refused to give the Mets an edge. Working around a Rolen throwing error that created a first-and-third situation with one out, Suppan intentionally walked Green, struck out Valentin, and induced Chavez to fly out to Edmonds to end the inning.

Wainwright allowed the first two batters to reach base on a pair of singles. But with runners on first and second, he buckled down and struck out pinch-hitter Cliff Floyd, then induced Reyes to hit a sharp fly ball to Edmonds. Lo Duca worked a walk to load the bases for Beltran. Three pitches later, Wainwright struck out Beltran on a beautiful curve ball to send the Cardinals to the World Series.

Bot 6th
STL 1
NYM 1

Bot 9th
STL 3
NYM 1

Top 9th
STL 3
NYM 1

Mets manager Willie Randolph stuck with reliever Aaron Heilman in the ninth instead of going to Wagner. After striking out Edmonds, Heilman gave up a single to Rolen after a nine-pitch battle. That brought up Molina, who, despite a poor regular season at the plate, had established himself as an offensive threat in the NLCS by collecting six hits, four RBIs, and a home run. On the first pitch he saw from Heilman, Molina delivered the biggest hit of his career, a two-run homer that landed just over the wall in the left-field bullpen.

RIGHT: Yadier Molina, Albert Pujols, and Adam Wainwright display the trophy for the NL pennant. AP/WWP
BELOW: Endy Chavez leaps to rob Scott Rolen of a home run in Game 7 of the NLCS. AP/WWP

WORLD SERIES

The World Series matchup was a shock to all of baseball: one team that no one expected to be in there at the start of the season pitted against another team that no one expected to be there by the end. For the Cardinals, it was time to make amends. The 2005 team didn't get the opportunity to say goodbye to old Busch Stadium in the manner they preferred, thanks in part to the right arm of Roy Oswalt. In 2006, the Cardinals made certain to welcome the new Busch Stadium with a warm embrace. Sellout after sellout during the regular season culminated in some of the most exciting September baseball St. Louis fans have ever seen. But that was just a prelude to the virtuoso performance the Cardinals were about to give in October—particularly in Games 3 through 5 of the World Series. On their home field, the Cardinals took advantage of the Tigers' sloppy fielding and jumped on the sturdy back of their inspired hurlers. The third incarnation of Busch Stadium wouldn't have to wait long for its first epic celebration. The Diehard Cards were about to put their stamp on a proud franchise by winning the elusive No. 10.

RIGHT: Tony La Russa embraces Tigers manager Jim Leyland prior to the start of Game 1 of the World Series. Jonathan Daniel/Getty Images
BELOW: A sea of red prepares to enter Busch Stadium prior to Game 3 of the World Series. Jamie Squire/Getty Images

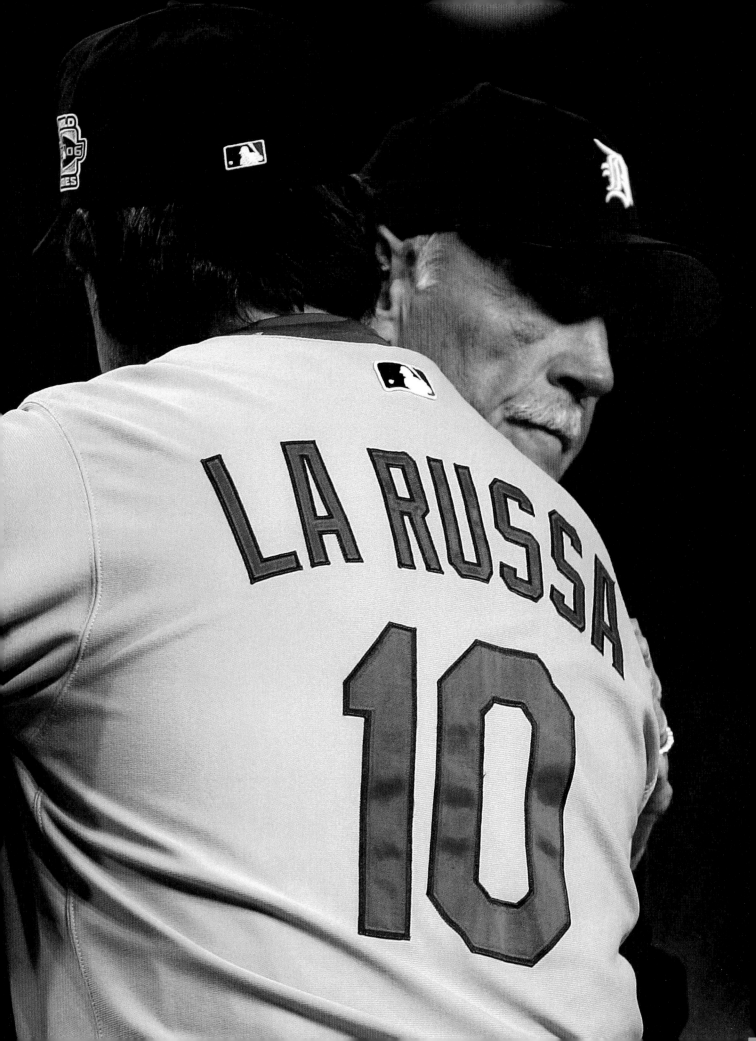

Much as they had done against the Mets, the Cards promptly responded to the Tigers' first-inning tally by evening the score, as Rolen took Justin Verlander deep—his first home run of the postseason.

Pujols walked to open the inning, then advanced to third on a wild pick-off throw by Verlander. Edmonds singled him home, and Rolen followed with a ground-rule double to put two runners in scoring position with no outs. Jason Grilli came on in relief, and was promptly plagued by an odd pairing of miscues. Encarnacion hit a grounder to third baseman Brandon Inge, who threw home in an attempt to get Edmonds at the plate. But Inge's throw sailed wide of Rodriguez, allowing Edmonds to score. Rolen came around third on the play and collided with Inge, who was standing in his way. Obstruction was called against Inge, and Rolen was allowed to score the inning's final run.

Top 2ⁿᵈ
STL 1
DET 1

Top 6ᵗʰ
STL 7
DET 1

Oct. 21
Game 1
@ DET
W, 7-2

Bot 1ˢᵗ
DET 1
STL 0

Top 3ʳᵈ
STL 4
DET 1

Molina singled to open the frame and was moved over to second on a ground out. After Eckstein struck out, Duncan doubled to right, and Pujols followed by hammering the first pitch he saw from Verlander over the right-field fence.

Anthony Reyes received a cold reception from the Tigers lineup in the first, as Craig Monroe doubled and was knocked in on a Carlos Guillen double three batters later. But with runners on first and third and two outs, Reyes was able to limit the damage to just one run by getting Ivan Rodriguez to line out to end the inning. From there, Reyes retired 17 straight batters and allowed just two more hits, one a home run to Monroe in the top of the ninth.

Anthony Reyes fires a pitch to the plate during Game 1 of the World Series. Jed Jacobsohn/Getty Images

St. Louis made things interesting with Tigers closer Todd Jones on the mound. With two outs, Rolen singled, took second without a throw, and moved to third on a fielding error by Jones that allowed Encarnacion to reach base. Edmonds then doubled to score Rolen and place the tying runs in scoring position for Wilson, who was hit by a pitch to load the bases. La Russa opted to stick with Molina at the plate instead of going to one of his lefty bats on the bench, and Jones earned the tough save by getting Molina to hit a ground ball to short for the game's final out.

Monroe hit his second solo home run of the series, and Guillen doubled in Magglio Ordonez to give Detroit all the runs they would need with Rogers on the mound.

Bot 1st
DET 2
STL 0

Top 9th
DET 3
STL 1

**Oct. 22
Game 2
@ DET
L, 3-1**

Top 1st
STL 0
DET 0

Bot 4th
DET 2
STL 0

During the top of the first, TV cameras focused in on a smudge on Kenny Rogers' left hand, and "Smudge-gate" was off and running. The Cardinals, unfortunately, were not. After the first inning, Rogers retired 20 of 23 batters he faced without allowing a runner to reach scoring position.

With runners on first and second and no one out, Weaver induced Ramon Santiago to pop up on the infield. Pujols charged on the play, but could not make the catch. The error loaded the bases with Curtis Granderson at the plate. Weaver responded with some of his best work of the postseason to get out of the inning unscathed. But in the bottom of the fifth, the Tigers finally capitalized with runners in scoring position. Sean Casey singled home Guillen to give Detroit a three-run lead.

Ronnie Belliard sported a new look prior to Game 1 of the World Series. Jonathan Daniel/Getty Images

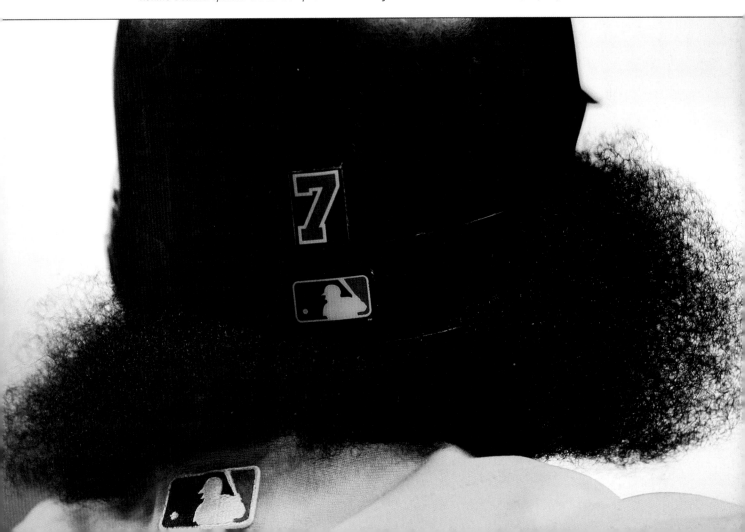

A pair of walks gave St. Louis another scoring opportunity in the seventh against Joel Zumaya. With Pujols at the plate, Zumaya got exactly what he wanted as Pujols hit a weak ball back to the pitcher. Zumaya turned and fired to third to get the lead runner, but his throw was wild and a diving Inge could not corral the errant throw. Both Eckstein and Wilson scored on the play to double the Cardinals' lead.

Bot 7th
STL 4
DET 0

Oct. 24
Game 3
DET
W, 5-0

Bot 4th
STL 2
DET 0

Top 8th
STL 4
DET 0

Wilson singled off Nate Robertson to start the inning. On a 3-1 pitch, Pujols hit a ground-rule double to right, which prevented Wilson from scoring. Rolen followed with a four-pitch walk; then Belliard hit into a fielder's choice, with the throw from Inge coming home to force Wilson out at the plate. Edmonds came up with one out and the bases still loaded, and pounded a double to right field to score the first two runs of the inning. Robertson regrouped to get the final two outs of the inning and keep the score 2-0 Cardinals.

Carpenter retired the side in order thanks to a double-play ground out to end the inning. With just 82 pitches thrown, Carpenter left after eight innings as the Cardinals tacked on an extra run in the bottom half of the inning. For the game, he allowed just three hits and no walks, while striking out six; only once did a runner reach scoring position, and six times Carpenter posted 1-2-3 innings. It was simply a magnificent performance.

LEFT: *A notable discoloration is visible on Kenny Rogers pitching hand in this photo from Game 2 of the World Series.* Jamie Squire/Getty Images
BELOW: *Chris Carpenter saved his best start of the postseason for Game 3 of the World Series.* Jamie Squire/Getty Images

A lead-off Granderson double and a one-out walk brought Casey to the plate, and he again got the best of Cardinals pitching with a single to score Granderson. Rodriguez then singled to right to score Guillen. Suppan got out of the jam by inducing Polanco to ground into a fielder's choice.

Top 3rd
DET 3
STL 0

Oct. 26
Game 4
DET
W, 5-4

Top 2nd
DET 1
STL 0

Bot 3rd
DET 3
STL 1

After sitting down the Tigers in order in the first, Suppan allowed a home run to Casey, then worked around a two-on, two-out situation to escape further damage.

Miles singled to center with one out, and then stole second on a close play. With two outs, Eckstein delivered with a double to score Miles and put the Cardinals on the board. Duncan followed with a walk, but Jeremy Bonderman retired Pujols on a ground out to end the inning.

Josh Kinney threw 6 1/3 scoreless innings in the postseason, and picked up the win in Game 2 of the NLCS. Ron Vesely/MLB Photos via Getty Images

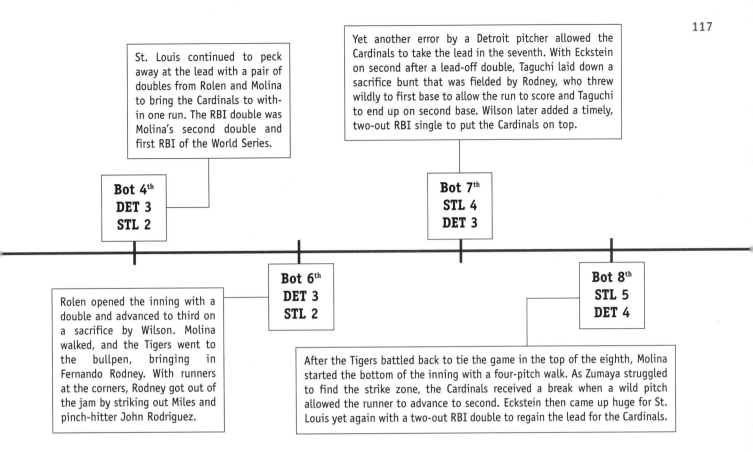

St. Louis continued to peck away at the lead with a pair of doubles from Rolen and Molina to bring the Cardinals to within one run. The RBI double was Molina's second double and first RBI of the World Series.

Yet another error by a Detroit pitcher allowed the Cardinals to take the lead in the seventh. With Eckstein on second after a lead-off double, Taguchi laid down a sacrifice bunt that was fielded by Rodney, who threw wildly to first base to allow the run to score and Taguchi to end up on second base. Wilson later added a timely, two-out RBI single to put the Cardinals on top.

Bot 4th
DET 3
STL 2

Bot 7th
STL 4
DET 3

Bot 6th
DET 3
STL 2

Bot 8th
STL 5
DET 4

Rolen opened the inning with a double and advanced to third on a sacrifice by Wilson. Molina walked, and the Tigers went to the bullpen, bringing in Fernando Rodney. With runners at the corners, Rodney got out of the jam by striking out Miles and pinch-hitter John Rodriguez.

After the Tigers battled back to tie the game in the top of the eighth, Molina started the bottom of the inning with a four-pitch walk. As Zumaya struggled to find the strike zone, the Cardinals received a break when a wild pitch allowed the runner to advance to second. Eckstein then came up huge for St. Louis yet again with a two-out RBI double to regain the lead for the Cardinals.

Preston Wilson makes a difficult catch to rob Craig Monroe of a hit in Game 4. Ron Vesely/MLB Photos via Getty Images

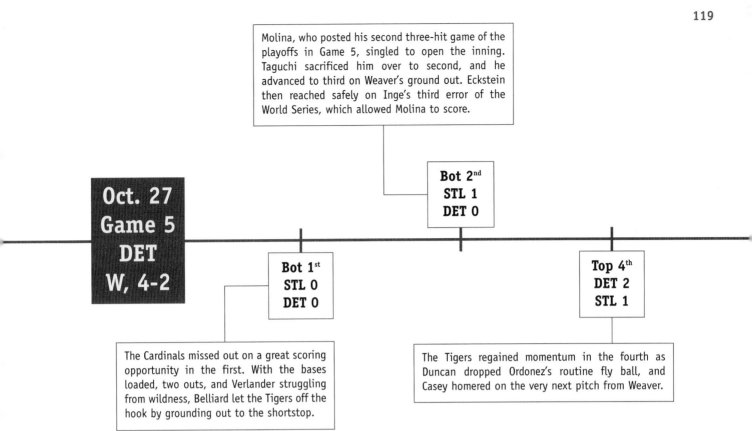

Molina, who posted his second three-hit game of the playoffs in Game 5, singled to open the inning. Taguchi sacrificed him over to second, and he advanced to third on Weaver's ground out. Eckstein then reached safely on Inge's third error of the World Series, which allowed Molina to score.

Bot 2ⁿᵈ
STL 1
DET 0

Oct. 27
Game 5
DET
W, 4-2

Bot 1ˢᵗ
STL 0
DET 0

Top 4ᵗʰ
DET 2
STL 1

The Cardinals missed out on a great scoring opportunity in the first. With the bases loaded, two outs, and Verlander struggling from wildness, Belliard let the Tigers off the hook by grounding out to the shortstop.

The Tigers regained momentum in the fourth as Duncan dropped Ordonez's routine fly ball, and Casey homered on the very next pitch from Weaver.

LEFT: Scott Rolen and Albert Pujols embrace on the field after the final out of the World Series. Rich Pilling/MLB Photos via Getty Images
BELOW: Albert Pujols celebrates with fans after Game 5 of the World Series. Jamie Squire/Getty Images

Pujols had not contributed much with his bat in the World Series, so in Game 5 he turned to his glove. He made an exceptional diving stop to his right on a ball hit by Placido Polanco, then threw to Weaver at first from a sitting position. Weaver stepped on the bag to record the first out of the inning just before Polanco touched the base. Weaver lasted eight impressive innings, fanning nine batters while allowing just four hits.

Top 7th
STL 3
DET 2

Bot 4th
STL 3
DET 2

Bot 9th
STL 4
DET 2

Verlander's throwing error—the fifth by a Tigers pitcher in the World Series—allowed a run to score and put runners on second and third for Eckstein, whose RBI ground out put St. Louis back on top.

Wainwright's first save of the World Series was a dramatic one. After surrendering a double and allowing the pinch-runner to advance to third on a wild pitch, Wainwright walked Polanco to put the tying run on base. Inge stepped to plate looking to redeem himself after all of his miscues in the field. Just as Wainwright had done against Beltran to end the NLCS, he struck out Inge on three consecutive pitches to clinch the St. Louis Cardinals' tenth World Series.

RIGHT: David Eckstein holds his World Series MVP trophy while sitting on the car he was awarded. Rich Pilling/MLB Photos via Getty Images
BELOW: David Eckstein enjoys some postgame libations after winning the World Series. Elsa/Getty Images

DATE	OPPONENT	SCORE	ST. LOUIS PITCHER OF RECORD	REC.	INSIDE THE BOX SCORE
April 3	@ Philadelphia	W 13-5	Carpenter (1-0)	1-0	8-run 4th powers Cards; Pujols (2 HR) and Rolen (1 HR) combine for 8 RBIs; Miles goes 4-for-5
April 5	@ Philadelphia	W 4-3	Thompson (1-0)	2-0	Pujols, Schumaker homer; Molina hits game-winning single in 9th to score Rolen
April 6	@ Philadelphia	W 4-2	Marquis (1-0)	3-0	Phils' Rollins sees hit streak end at 38 games; Marquis effective, Isringhausen picks up 2nd save
April 7	@ Chi. Cubs	L 5-1	Suppan (0-1)	3-1	Lee homers, Maddux cruises through 6-plus innings as Cards limited to just 4 hits
April 8	@ Chi. Cubs	L 3-2	Thompson (1-1)	3-2	Carpenter (6 IP, 4 H, 0 ER, 9 SO) outduels Zambrano, but pen surrenders HR to Barrett and Lee
April 9	@ Chi. Cubs	L 8-4	Isringhausen (0-1)	3-3	Barrett's grand slam off Isringhausen sinks Cards; Rolen goes 3-for-4 with HR, 2 RBIs
April 10	Milwaukee	W 6-4	Mulder (1-0)	4-3	Pujols hits 1st Cards HR at new Busch; Mulder pitches well (8 IP, 7 H, 2 ER, 5 SO) and homers
April 12	Milwaukee	W 8-3	Marquis (2-0)	5-3	Brewers shoddy defense, Edmonds bases-loaded double sparks 4-run 5th
April 13	Milwaukee	L 4-3 (11)	Isringhausen (0-2)	5-4	Lee's game-saving catches, game-winning HR in 11th off Isringhausen clinch game for Brewers
April 14	Cincinnati	L 1-0	Carpenter (1-1)	5-5	Harang hits (1 RBI) and pitches Reds to victory in duel with Carpenter (8 IP, 4 H, 1 ER, 6 SO)
April 15	Cincinnati	W 9-3	Ponson (1-0)	6-5	Ponson solid in home debut; Pujols, Spiezio, and Luna (3 RBIs) all homer
April 16	Cincinnati	W 8-7	Looper (1-0)	7-5	Pujols' three HR (including walkoff in 9th) and 5 RBIs power Cards to victory
April 17	@ Pittsburgh	W 2-1	Marquis (3-0)	8-5	Pujols ties MLB record with HR in 4th consecutive at-bat; Marquis solid (8 IP, 3 H, 1 ER)
April 18	@ Pittsburgh	L 12-4	Suppan (0-2)	8-6	Pujols hits 10th HR, but Pirates clobber Suppan (2 IP, 8 ER), bullpen
April 19	@ Pittsburgh	W 4-0	Carpenter (2-1)	9-6	Carpenter brilliant (8 IP, 2 H, 1 BB, 6 SO); Edmonds (3 RBIs) and Eckstein both homer
April 21	Chi. Cubs	W 9-3	Mulder (2-0)	10-6	Pujols (HR, 2B, 4 RBIs) collects 1,000 career hit; Mulder goes 8 strong innings
April 22	Chi. Cubs	W 4-1	Ponson (2-0)	11-6	Pujols' bases-loaded single in 5th gives Cards win; Ponson, bullpen impress
April 23	Chi. Cubs	L 7-3	Marquis (3-1)	11-7	Jones, Ramirez get best of Marquis as Maddux (7 IP, 5 H, 0 ER, 4 SO) rolls
April 24	Pittsburgh	W 7-2	Carpenter (3-1)	12-7	Pujols' homer off Oliver Perez leaves him one shy of MLB April record
April 25	Pittsburgh	W 6-3	Suppan (1-2)	13-7	Encarnacion collects 4 RBIs, falls a single short of hitting for cycle; Suppan effective for 7 IP
April 26	Pittsburgh	W 4-3	Isringhausen (1-2)	14-7	Isringhausen blows save on Hernandez HR; Pujols singles in Eckstein in bottom 9th for win
April 27	Washington	W 6-2	Ponson (3-0)	15-7	Edmonds' 3-run HR, Spiezio's 2-run 2B put game out of reach for Nationals
April 28	Washington	L 8-3	Marquis (3-2)	15-8	Pujols' record-tying 13th HR in April not enough; Marquis roughed up for 7 ER in 5 IP
April 29	Washington	W 2-1	Looper (2-0)	16-8	Pujols hits game-winning, record-breaking HR in 8th; Carpenter, pen combine for solid game
April 30	Washington	W 9-2	Suppan (2-2)	17-8	Cards set club record with 17th April win; Taguchi, Edmonds each drive in 3 runs

April record: 17-8 (.680)	Place in NL Central: 1st (tied with Reds)	Runs scored: 125	Runs allowed: 93	Longest wining streak: 4	Longest losing streak: 3

DATE	OPPONENT	SCORE	ST. LOUIS PITCHER OF RECORD	REC.	INSIDE THE BOX SCORE
May 1	@ Cincinnati	L 6-1	Mulder (2-1)	17-9	Arroyo dominates Cards, tosses complete game, 4-hitter; Encarnacion HR Cards only tally
May 2	@ Cincinnati	L 3-2	Falkenborg (0-1)	17-10	Javier Valentin singles in winning run in bottom 9th; Cards fall 2 games back of Reds in Central
May 3	@ Houston	L 5-4	Marquis (3-3)	17-11	Spiezio, Luna, Pujols' HR not enough for Cards; Lidge shaky, but retires Pujols, notches save
May 4	@ Houston	L 4-3	Carpenter (3-2)	17-12	Berkman's 4th and 5th RBIs of series give Pettitte win over Carpenter
May 5	@ Florida	W 7-2	Suppan (3-2)	18-12	Pujols' 16th HR sparks 7-run 5th inning for Cards; Suppan cruises through 8-plus innings
May 6	@ Florida	W 7-6	Mulder (3-1)	19-12	Cards rough up Willis for 12 hits in 4-plus IP to give Mulder his 100th career win
May 7	@ Florida	W 9-1	Hancock (1-0)	20-12	Cards score 5 runs in 4th, post 6 solid innings of relief to sweep Marlins
May 8	Colorado	L 6-2	Marquis (3-4)	20-13	Holliday homers twice off Marquis; Cards can't figure out Francis
May 9	Colorado	W 4-2	Wainwright (1-0)	21-13	Pujols hits game-winning, 3-run HR in 8th; Isringhausen strikes out side in perfect 9th
May 10	Colorado	W 7-4	Suppan (4-2)	22-13	Pujols fastest ever to 18 HR; Cards collect 13 hits, Cards still trail Reds by 0.5 games
May 12	Arizona	W 5-3	Mulder (4-1)	23-13	Edmonds HR, 3 RBIs power Cards to win, tie with Reds for 1st
May 13	Arizona	W 9-1	Marquis (4-4)	24-13	Pujols, Edmonds, Rolen combine for 7 H, 6 R, 9 RBIs; Marquis good (7 IP, 3 H, 1 ER)
May 14	Arizona	L 7-6	Wainwright (1-1)	24-14	Pen, errors waste Carpenter's strong start; despite loss, Cards maintain 1 game lead in Central
May 16	NY Mets	L 8-3	Suppan (4-3)	24-15	Lo Duca RBI double off Suppan breaks 7th-inning tie; Glavine gets 6th win
May 17	NY Mets	W 1-0	Mulder (5-1)	25-15	Rolen 2B scores Pujols in 6th; Mulder dominates (8 IP, 4 H, 2 BB, 5 SO)
May 18	NY Mets	W 6-3	Marquis (5-4)	26-15	Pujols gets day off; Eckstein (3-for-4, 2 R, 2 RBIs) and Spiezio (2 RBIs) pace Cards
May 19	@ Kansas City	W 9-6	Carpenter (4-2)	27-15	Royals pounce on Carpenter early, but Pujols' 20th HR, Spiezio's hot bat rally Cards
May 20	@ Kansas City	W 4-2	Reyes (1-0)	28-15	Pujols homers again and Reyes wins 2006 debut as Cards lead grows to 3 in Central
May 21	@ Kansas City	W 10-3	Suppan (5-3)	29-15	Pujols homers in 3rd-straight game; Duncan gets 1st HR of year; Cards sweep Royals
May 22	@ San Fran.	L 9-2	Mulder (5-2)	29-16	Streaking Giants score 6 in 8th off Johnson and Looper to seal win
May 23	@ San Fran.	W 8-5	Marquis (6-4)	30-16	Pujols 3-run HR in 1st off Matt Morris gives Cards lead they never surrender
May 24	@ San Fran.	W 10-4	Wainwright (2-1)	31-16	Wainwright homers in first MLB at-bat; Cards pitchers combine to fall single short of cycle
May 26	@ San Diego	L 7-1	Suppan (5-4)	31-17	Padres hitters—led by HRs from Roberts, Piazza, and Gonzalez—jump on Suppan early
May 27	@ San Diego	W 4-3	Ponson (4-0)	32-17	Molina picks off Giles at 1st base in bottom of 9th to end game
May 28	@ San Diego	L 10-8	Mulder (5-3)	32-18	Bellhorn hits longest HR in Petco history off Mulder as Padres win slugfest feat. 6 HRs
May 29	Houston	W 3-1	Marquis (7-4)	33-18	Pujols hits 3-run, game-winning HR off Qualls in 7th; Marquis impresses (7 IP, 3 H, 1 ER)
May 30	Houston	L 6-3	Hancock (1-1)	33-19	Stros rally to score 5 in 7th off Reyes, Hancock; Rolen, Encarnacion both homer
May 31	Houston	W 4-3 (11)	Looper (3-0)	34-19	Taguchi's bases-loaded, 2-out single wins game for Cards in bottom of 11th

May record: 17-11 (.607)	Place in NL Central: 1st (5 ahead of Reds)	Runs scored: 142	Runs allowed: 120	Longest wining streak: 5	Longest losing streak: 4

DATE	OPPONENT	SCORE	ST. LOUIS PITCHER OF RECORD	REC.	INSIDE THE BOX SCORE
June 2	Chi. Cubs	L 5-4 (14)	Hancock (1-2)	34-20	Walker's grounder scoots through Rolen's legs to tie game in 9th; Cubs win in 14th on Walker RBI
June 3	Chi. Cubs	L 8-5	Mulder (5-4)	34-21	Pujols strains right oblique muscle; Ramirez grand slam in 4th knocks Mulder, Cards out of game
June 4	Chi. Cubs	W 9-6	Marquis (8-4)	35-21	Encarnacion, Rolen, Edmonds combine for 4 doubles, 7 RBIs to help Cards avoid sweep
June 5	Cincinnati	L 8-7	Isringhausen (1-3)	35-22	Griffey's 3-run HR off Isringhausen in 9th—his 2nd of game—clinches comeback for Reds
June 6	Cincinnati	L 7-0	Carpenter (4-3)	35-23	Milton's 7 scoreless innings and Reds' 15 hits topple Carpenter, ineffective pen
June 7	Cincinnati	L 7-4	Ponson (4-1)	35-24	Reds KO Ponson as Aurilla collects 5 RBIs; Reds sweep, tie cards in standings
June 9	@ Milwaukee	W 10-6	Hancock (2-2)	36-24	Brewers score 6 in first two frames off Mulder, but Cards rally for 6 in 4th to take back lead
June 10	@ Milwaukee	L 4-3	Flores (0-1)	36-25	Pen can't hold lead; Hart's pinch-hit single scores winning run in 8th off Looper

DATE	OPPONENT	SCORE	ST. LOUIS PITCHER OF RECORD	REC.	INSIDE THE BOX SCORE
June 11	@ Milwaukee	W 7-5	Hancock (3-2)	37-25	Brewers hit 3 solo homers off Suppan, but pen pitches 5 scoreless innings for win
June 13	@ Pittsburgh	W 2-1	Carpenter (5-3)	38-25	Carpenter (7 IP, 3 H, 0 ER, 13 SO) outduels Oliver Perez as Cards lead in Central grows to 3
June 14	@ Pittsburgh	L 9-7	Ponson (4-2)	38-26	Cards 9th-inning rally too little, too late; Ponson allows 6 ER in 3-plus innings
June 15	@ Pittsburgh	W 6-5	Mulder (6-4)	39-26	Duncan's triple, double key Cards comeback win; Eckstein suffers concussion
June 16	Colorado	W 8-1	Marquis (9-4)	40-26	Marquis goes 8 strong innings for 9th win; Luna drives in 2 during key 6-run 8th inning
June 17	Colorado	W 6-5	Suppan (6-4)	41-26	Encarnacion wallops 2 homers to spark offense and help Suppan pick up 100th career win
June 18	Colorado	W 4-1	Carpenter (6-3)	42-26	Cardinals climb to season-high 16 games over .500 as Rolen homers for 9th time to finish sweep
June 20	@ Chi. White Sox	L 20-6	Mulder (6-5)	42-27	11-run 3rd inning leads to 24 hits and most runs scored in a game against a La Russa-managed team
June 21	@ Chi. White Sox	L 13-5	Marquis (9-5)	42-28	Marquis allows 13 runs and 14 hits in only 5 IP; Edmonds leaves game with concussion
June 22	@ Chi. White Sox	L 1-0	Reyes (1-1)	42-29	Sox sweep thanks to Thome HR despite one-hitter from Reyes, who struck out 6 and walked none
June 23	@ Detroit	L 10-6	Carpenter (6-4)	42-30	Pujols, Rolen combine for 7 hits but only one RBI as Carpenter gives up 7 runs and 9 hits
June 24	@ Detroit	L 7-6 (10)	Johnson (0-1)	42-31	Marcus Thames hits 2-run homer in 9th to tie it, Polanco wins it in 10th with RBI double
June 25	@ Detroit	L 4-1	Ponson (4-3)	42-32	Curtis Granderson keys 3-run 8th inning for Tigers as they complete sweep over punchless Cards
June 26	Cleveland	L 10-3	Marquis (9-6)	42-33	Travis Hafner homers twice to fuel big win; Rolen and Taguchi collect 3 hits and an RBI in loss
June 27	Cleveland	L 3-1	Reyes (1-2)	42-34	C.C. Sabathia stymies Cards for 8 innings; team loses 8th in a row for first time since 1988
June 28	Cleveland	W 5-4	Isringhausen (2-3)	43-34	A pair of Tribe errors in 9th allow comeback victory as Cards losing streak ends
June 30	Kansas City	L 7-5 (10)	Looper (3-1)	43-35	2 runs in 10th lead come-from-behind win for Royals; Doug Mientkiewicz homers and drives in 3
June record: 9-16 (.360)		Place in NL Central: 1st (tied with Reds)		Runs scored: 120	Runs allowed: 157 — Longest wining streak: 4 — Longest losing streak: 8
July 1	Kansas City	L 8-7 (11)	Isringhausen (2-4)	43-36	Cardinals pitchers walk 10 Royals; Mark Teahen drives in 4 for KC in another extra-inning win
July 2	Kansas City	W 9-7	Marquis (10-6)	44-36	Pujols, Edmonds, Rolen all homer; Marquis picks up 10th win as Cardinals avoid KC sweep
July 3	@ Atlanta	L 6-3	Reyes (1-3)	44-37	Braves homer four times while Smoltz out-pitches rookie Reyes; Pujols hits 28th homer in loss
July 4	@ Atlanta	W 6-3	Carpenter (7-4)	45-37	Encarnacion's 2-run homer powers Cardinals to rain-soaked win; ends 7-game road losing streak
July 5	@ Atlanta	L 14-4	Suppan (6-5)	45-38	Suppan gives up career-high 10 runs in blowout; Rolen/Luna homers Cards' only highlights
July 6	@ Houston	L 4-2	Ponson (4-4)	45-39	Edmonds hits 2-run homer but Ponson loses 4th in a row; Cards' 8th-innng rally squashed by Lidge
July 7	@ Houston	W 8-2	Marquis (11-6)	46-39	Strong pitching from Marquis and 3-run 9th inning ice win; Ponson designated for assignment
July 8	@ Houston	W 7-6 (10)	Isringhausen (3-4)	47-39	2-out, 2-run rally in 9th off Lidge ties game; Pujols HR off Oswalt in 10th wins it
July 9	@ Houston	W 7-5 (12)	Looper (4-1)	48-39	Astros tie game in 9th off Isringhausen; Miles 2-run 2B in 12th off Lidge wins game
July 13	Los Angeles	W 3-2 (14)	Looper (5-1)	49-39	Marquis, relievers pitch well; Edmonds HR ties game in 7th; Pujols' 30th HR a game-winner in 14th
July 14	Los Angeles	W 5-0	Carpenter (8-4)	50-39	Carpenter two-hits L.A. in complete game shutout; Duncan, Encarnacion both collect HR, 2 RBIs
July 15	Los Angeles	W 2-1 (10)	Looper (6-1)	51-39	Suppan pitches 7 strong innings; Rolen hits game-winning single in 10th to score Eckstein
July 16	Los Angeles	W 11-3	Reyes (2-3)	52-39	Pujols goes 4-for-5 with 2 2B, 3 RBIs; Duncan 3-for-4 with 3 runs; Molina 3-for-4, 2 2B, 3 RBIs
July 17	Atlanta	L 15-3	Weaver (0-1)	52-40	Braves pound Weaver in his St. Louis debut, collect 20 hits; Cards win streak ends at 7
July 18	Atlanta	L 14-5	Marquis (11-7)	52-41	Andruw Jones unstoppable: 5-for-5 with 2 HR, 6 RBIs; Marquis surrenders 12 runs in 5 IP
July 19	Atlanta	W 8-3	Carpenter (9-4)	53-41	Carpenter tames Braves bats over 7 IP; Cards score 4 runs in 3rd and 5th
July 21	@ Los Angeles	W 2-0	Suppan (7-5)	54-41	Suppan impresses (7 IP, 5 H, 0 ER); Wainwright, Isringhausen finish off L.A.; Duncan homers
July 22	@ Los Angeles	W 6-1	Weaver (1-1)	55-41	Cards tie franchise mark, HR in 18th straight game; Weaver gets 1st Cards win (5.2 IP, 6 H, 1 ER)
July 23	@ Los Angeles	W 6-1	Marquis (12-7)	56-41	Cards sweep season series vs. L.A.; Encarnacion homers twice; Marquis cruises (8 IP, 4 H, 0 ER)
July 24	@ Colorado	L 7-0	Reyes (2-4)	56-42	Rockies pound Reyes; Jeff Francis takes perfect game into 6th, settles for 2-hitter with 8 Ks
July 25	@ Colorado	W 1-0	Carpenter (10-4)	57-42	Pujols HR in 6th the difference; Carpenter outduels Jason Jennings; Isringhausen earns 28th save
July 26	@ Colorado	W 6-1	Suppan (8-5)	58-42	Big day at the plate for Edmonds, Miles, Rodriguez; Suppan posts 3rd-straight quality start
July 27	@ Chi. Cubs	L 5-4	Johnson (0-2)	58-43	Cubs two-out rally in 6th against Weaver, pen cost Cards the game
July 28	@ Chi. Cubs	L 6-5	Marquis (12-8)	58-44	Rolen's error gives Cubs new life in 4th; Pierre takes advantage with game-winning 3-RBI triple
July 29	@ Chi. Cubs	L 4-2	Reyes (2-5)	58-45	Cards' 9th-inning, two-out rally falls short as Dempster Ks Miles, bases left loaded
July 30	@ Chi. Cubs	L 6-3	Carpenter (10-5)	58-46	Cubs rough up Carpenter early in his shortest start of season (4 IP, 6 H, 5 ER); Zambrano wins duel
July record: 15-11 (.577)		Place in NL Central: 1st (3.5 ahead of Reds)		Runs scored: 125	Runs allowed: 124 — Longest wining streak: 7 — Longest losing streak: 4
Aug. 1	Philadelphia	L 5-3	Suppan (8-6)	58-47	Belliard goes 0-for-4 with error in Cards debut; Sosa pitches scoreless frame in Cards debut
Aug. 2	Philadelphia	L 16-8	Weaver (1-2)	58-48	Phillies pummel Weaver, Cards pen for 18 hits—including 4 HR—and 16 runs
Aug. 3	Philadelphia	L 8-1	Marquis (12-9)	58-49	Utley extends hit streak to 35 games as Cards get swept; Cole Hamels dominates (7 IP, 2 H, 12 SO)
Aug. 4	Milwaukee	L 4-3	Carpenter (10-6)	58-50	Cards post 2nd 8-game losing streak of season; Carpenter exits early batted ball hits his thumb
Aug. 5	Milwaukee	W 4-3	Reyes (3-5)	59-50	Edmonds' amazing catch robs Prince Fielder of a bases-loaded hit in the 6th to preserve lead
Aug. 6	Milwaukee	W 7-1	Suppan (9-6)	60-50	Encarnacion hits 3-run HR and Pujols goes 3-for-4; Suppan (7.1 IP, 4 H, 7 SO) baffles Brewers
Aug. 7	@ Cincinnati	W 13-1	Weaver (2-2)	61-50	Cards score 5 in top of 1st, enjoy rout; hitters combine for 10 extra-base hits; Weaver impresses
Aug. 8	@ Cincinnati	L 10-3	Marquis (12-10)	61-51	Reds answer previous loss with 17 hits of their own; Marquis horrible (2.2 IP, 9 H, 4 ER)
Aug. 9	@ Cincinnati	L 8-7	Isringhausen (3-5)	61-52	Slugfest ends in defeat with walk-off HR for David Ross; 8th blown save of year for Isringhausen
Aug. 10	@ Cincinnati	W 6-1	Reyes (4-5)	62-52	Cards split series, remain 3.5 games ahead of Reds; Duncan homers twice
Aug. 11	@ Pittsburgh	L 7-1	Suppan (9-7)	62-53	Pirates lefty Zach Duke tosses complete game; Pujols goes 4-4 with 3 doubles
Aug. 12	@ Pittsburgh	L 3-2	Weaver (2-3)	62-54	Pujols hits 35th HR—a 2-run shot—but rest of team musters just 4 hits against Ian Snell
Aug. 13	@ Pittsburgh	L 7-0	Marquis (12-11)	62-55	Cards suffer sweep against last-place Pirates; Wainwright gives us 4 runs, gets just one out in relief
Aug. 15	Cincinnati	W 5-0	Carpenter (11-6)	63-55	Carpenter dominates in complete game, 4-hit gem; Edmonds leaves game with dizziness
Aug. 16	Cincinnati	L 7-2	Reyes (4-6)	63-56	Reds hit 5 HR off Reyes, Sosa; Arroyo shines through 7 for Cincinnati
Aug. 17	Cincinnati	W 2-1	Isringhausen (4-5)	64-56	Cards take series, increase lead to 2.5 games over Reds; Weaver impresses (7.1 IP, 3 H, 1 ER)
Aug. 18	@ Chi. Cubs	W 11-3	Marquis (13-11)	65-56	Cards clobber Cubs with 5 HRs; Wilson goes 2-for-5 with a HR in his Cards debut
Aug. 19	@ Chi. Cubs	L 5-4 (10)	Isringhausen (4-6)	65-57	Belliard ties game with 2B in 9th; Isringhausen surrenders bases-loaded hit to Nevin in 10th for loss

DATE	OPPONENT	SCORE	ST. LOUIS PITCHER OF RECORD	REC.	INSIDE THE BOX SCORE
Aug. 20	@ Chi. Cubs	W 5-3	Carpenter (12-6)	66-57	Carpenter cruises through 8; Isringhausen gives up Ramirez HR in 9th but holds on for 30th save
Aug. 22	@ NY Mets	L 8-7	Isringhausen (4-7)	66-58	Pujols (7 RBI), Delgado (5 RBI) both homer twice, hit grand slams; Beltran hits walk-off HR in 9th
Aug. 23	@ NY Mets	L 10-8	Mulder (6-6)	66-59	Returning from lengthy DL stint, Mulder gets tagged for 9 runs, 9 hits, and 4 walks in 3 IP
Aug. 24	@ NY Mets	L 6-2	Marquis (13-12)	66-60	Mets complete sweep, hammer Marquis (6 IP, 7 H, 4 BB, 5 ER)
Aug. 25	Chi. Cubs	W 2-0	Suppan (10-7)	67-60	Suppan brilliant (7.2 IP, 5 H, 2 SO); Belliard, Bennett, and Suppan go 7-for-10 at plate
Aug. 26	Chi. Cubs	W 2-1	Flores (1-1)	68-60	Carpenter silences Cubs (8 IP, 2 H, 1 ER, 9 SO); Bennett HRs, then hits game-winning single in 9th
Aug. 27	Chi. Cubs	W 10-6	Looper (7-1)	69-60	Bennett hits 2-out, grand slam in bottom of 9th off Howry to complete sweep of Cubs in wild game
Aug. 29	Florida	L 9-1	Mulder (6-7)	69-61	Mulder rocked again, done for year; Marlins pound out 15 hits against Cards
Aug. 30	Florida	W 13-6	Marquis (14-12)	70-61	Cards end Florida's 9-game win streak thanks to big day from big boppers, season-best 20 hits
Aug. 31	Florida	W 5-2	Looper (8-1)	71-61	Suppan, Willis hook up in 7-inning pitcher's duel; Cards win with 4-run 8th

August record: 13-15 (.464)   Place in NL Central: 1st (5 ahead of Reds)   Runs scored: 137   Runs allowed: 141   Longest winning streak: 3   Longest losing streak: 4

DATE	OPPONENT	SCORE	ST. LOUIS PITCHER OF RECORD	REC.	INSIDE THE BOX SCORE
Sept. 1	Pittsburgh	W 3-1	Carpenter (13-6)	72-61	Carpenter's 3-hitter dispenses of the Pirates for the fourth time in '06 in just 1 hour, 54 minutes
Sept. 2	Pittsburgh	L 1-0	Weaver (2-4)	72-62	Ronny Paulino's bases-loaded sac fly the game's only run; Weaver loses (7 IP, 5 H, 1 ER, 4 SO)
Sept. 3	Pittsburgh	W 6-3	Reyes (5-6)	73-62	Pujols homers in 1st 3 at-bats, collects 5 RBI; Reyes pitches well (6.1 IP, 4 H, 0 ER, 9 SO)
Sept. 4	@ Washington	L 4-1	Marquis (14-13)	73-63	Ramon Ortiz comes within 3 outs of no-hitter; Pujols hits 43rd HR in 9th
Sept. 5	@ Washington	W 2-0	Suppan (11-7)	74-63	Pujols solo HR all the help Suppan needs (7.2 IP, 5 H, 5 SO); Isringhausen gets his last save of '06
Sept. 6	@ Washington	L 7-6	Isringhausen (4-8)	74-64	After Wilson's 2-run HR gives Cards lead in 9th, Isringhausen blows 10th save, loses game
Sept. 7	@ Arizona	W 6-2	Weaver (3-4)	75-64	Spiezio homers twice, drives in 3 as Weaver, pen roll without Isringhausen
Sept. 8	@ Arizona	L 13-1	Reyes (5-7)	75-65	Cards can't score, can't stop D-backs from scoring in rout
Sept. 9	@ Arizona	L 3-0	Marquis (14-14)	75-66	Brandon Webb makes his Cy Young case with one-hitter (9 IP, 0 BB, 5 SO)
Sept. 10	@ Arizona	L 9-7	Sosa (3-11)	75-67	Tony Clark, Eric Byrnes hit back-to-back HRs off Sosa in 8th to break 7-7 tie
Sept. 11	Houston	W 7-0	Carpenter (14-6)	76-67	Carpenter pitches complete game, six-hitter; Belliard collects 4 RBIs to lead offense
Sept. 12	Houston	W 6-5	Looper (9-1)	77-67	Pujols 2-run 2B in bottom 9th off Lidge a game-winner; Looper gets 9th win of season
Sept. 13	Houston	L 5-1	Marquis (14-15)	77-68	Oswalt pitches 8 solid innings; Berkman 3-for-4 with HR, 2B
Sept. 15	San Francisco	W 14-4	Suppan (12-7)	78-68	Rolen goes 3-for-4 with 2B, 2 HR, 7 RBI; Duncan HRs twice, drives in 4
Sept. 16	San Francisco	W 6-1	Carpenter (15-6)	79-68	4-run 1st does in Matt Morris as Cards cruise; Pujols 4-for-4; Carpenter gets 100th career win
Sept. 17	San Francisco	postponed			
Sept. 18	@ Milwaukee	L 4-3	Looper (9-2)	79-69	Graffanino singles in winning run in 9th off Looper; Pujols hits 3-run HR (46)
Sept. 19	@ Milwaukee	W 12-2	Weaver (4-4)	80-69	Miles goes 4-for-6 with 3 RBI; Belliard 3-for-4 with 3 runs; Isringhausen opts for surgery
Sept. 20	@ Milwaukee	L 1-0	Johnson (0-3)	80-70	After getting 17 hits the day before, Cards muster just 4; Jenkins hits walk-off HR off Johnson
Sept. 21	@ Houston	L 6-5	Carpenter (15-7)	80-71	Berkman HRs twice off Carpenter, 2nd one a game-winner in 8th
Sept. 22	@ Houston	L 6-5	Looper (9-3)	80-72	Astros score 2 in 8th, 2 in 9th to rally against Wainwright, Johnson, Looper
Sept. 23	@ Houston	L 7-4	Johnson (0-4)	80-73	Cards take lead in top 9th; Luke Scott's 2nd HR of day a 3-run game-winner in bottom 9th
Sept. 24	@ Houston	L 7-3	Hancock (3-3)	80-74	Astros complete sweep with 4-run 7th as pen collapses again; Houston pulls to within 3.5 games
Sept. 25	San Diego	L 6-5	Thompson (1-2)	80-75	Piazza breaks tie with RBI single in 7th; Duncan hits 21st HR; Cards drop 6th straight;
Sept. 26	San Diego	L 7-5	Carpenter (15-8)	80-76	Carpenter blows 3-run lead, surrenders season-high 12 hits; Belliard homers twice
Sept. 27	San Diego	W 4-2	Johnson (1-4)	81-76	Cards come back with 3 runs in 8th off Pujols HR to halt skid; Wainwright gets 1st save since May
Sept. 28	Milwaukee	L 9-4	Marquis (14-16)	81-77	Marquis gets shelled (2 IP, 5 H, 3 BB, 6 ER) as division lead shrinks to half game
Sept. 29	Milwaukee	W 10-5	Weaver (5-4)	82-77	5-run 5th sparked by Pujols 3-run HR; Encarnacion, Rolen combine to go 7-for-10 with 5 runs
Sept. 30	Milwaukee	W 3-2	Johnson (2-4)	83-77	Spiezio's pinch-hit 3-run triple in 8th wins game, keeps Cards 1.5 game lead intact

September record: 12-16 (.429)   Place in NL Central: 1st (1.5 ahead of Astros)   Runs scored: 129   Runs allowed: 122   Longest winning streak: 2   Longest losing streak: 7

DATE	OPPONENT	SCORE	ST. LOUIS PITCHER OF RECORD	REC.	INSIDE THE BOX SCORE
Oct. 1	Milwaukee	L 5-3	Reyes (5-8)	83-78	Cards lose, but clinch division crown as Astros lose, too; Duncan, Pujols, Spiezio all HR in 9th

NATIONAL LEAGUE DIVISION SERIES

DATE	OPPONENT	SCORE	ST. LOUIS PITCHER OF RECORD	REC.	INSIDE THE BOX SCORE
Oct. 3	@ San Diego	W 5-1	Carpenter (1-0)	1-0	Pujols HRs, Cards rough up Jake Peavy; Carpenter cruises (6.1 IP, 5 H, 1 ER, 7 SO)
Oct. 5	@ San Diego	W 2-0	Weaver (1-0)	2-0	Wilson, Edmonds, and Pujols provided the offense; Weaver outpitched Wells; pen effective
Oct. 7	San Diego	L 3-1	Suppan (0-1)	2-1	Cards can't overcome Padres 3-run 4th as Chris Young dominates; Taguchi hits pinch-hit HR
Oct. 8	San Diego	W 6-2	Carpenter (2-)	3-1	Carpenter out-pitches Woody Williams; Belliard, Spiezio fuel offense as Cards advance to NLCS

NATIONAL LEAGUE CHAMPIONSHIP SERIES

DATE	OPPONENT	SCORE	ST. LOUIS PITCHER OF RECORD	REC.	INSIDE THE BOX SCORE
Oct. 11	@ NY Mets	postponed			
Oct. 12	@ NY Mets	L 2-0	Glavine (2-0)	3-2	Glavine dominates for 7 IP; Weaver (5.2 IP, 4 H, 2 ER), bullpen solid in loss
Oct. 13	@ NY Mets	W 9-6	Kinney (1-0)	4-2	St. Louis mounts rallies in the 7th and 9th to come from behind; Spiezio, Taguchi star for Cards
Oct. 14	NY Mets	W 5-0	Suppan (1-1)	5-2	Suppan pitches a gem (8 IP, 3 H, 0 ER, 4 SO) and hits a HR
Oct. 15	NY Mets	L 12-5	Thompson (0-1)	5-3	Cards relievers allow 10 runs; Eckstein, Edmonds, Molina all homer in loss
Oct. 16	NY Mets	postponed			
Oct. 17	NY Mets	W 4-2	Weaver (2-1)	6-3	Weaver goes six strong innings; Wainwright gets first NLCS save; Pujols, Duncan HR
Oct. 18	@ NY Mets	L 4-2	Carpenter (2-1)	6-4	John Maine pitches 5-plus shutout innings; Carpenter shaky through 6 IP
Oct. 19	@ NY Mets	W 3-1	Flores (1-0)	7-4	Molina's 9th-inning 2-run HR a series-winner; Suppan brilliant (7 IP, 2 H, 1 ER, 2 SO)

WORLD SERIES

DATE	OPPONENT	SCORE	ST. LOUIS PITCHER OF RECORD	REC.	INSIDE THE BOX SCORE
Oct. 21	@ Detroit	W 7-2	Reyes (1-0)	8-4	Reyes dominates (8 IP, 4 H, 2 ER, 4 SO); Rolen, Pujols HR
Oct. 22	@ Detroit	L 3-1	Rogers (3-0)	8-5	Rogers silences Cardinals with 8 shutout IP; critics question smudge on his hand
Oct. 24	Detroit	W 5-0	Carpenter (3-1)	9-5	Carpenter impresses (8 IP, 3 H, 0 ER, 6 SO); Cards bats come alive
Oct. 25	Detroit	postponed			
Oct. 26	Detroit	W 5-4	Wainwright (1-0)	10-5	Cards win back-and-forth battle; Eckstein goes 4-for-5 with 2 RBIs
Oct. 27	Detroit	W 4-2	Weaver (3-2)	11-5	Weaver nearly goes distance (8 IP, 4 H, 9 SO); Molina 3-for-4, 2 R; Eckstein named MVP

2006 Player Stats

Pitching

GS — Games started	CG — Complete games	IP — Innings pitched
SV — Saves	P/IP — Pitches per inning pitched	
BAA — Batting average against	WHIP — Walks + hits per inning pitched	

Chris Carpenter
Pitcher
Bats: Right   Throws: Right

	G	GS	CG	IP	H	R	ER	HR	BB	SO	W	L	SV	P/IP	BAA	WHIP	ERA
Season	32	32	5	221.2	194	81	76	21	43	184	15	8	0	14.7	.235	1.07	3.09
Playoffs	5	5	0	32.1	28	10	10	3	8	23	3	1	0	14.3	.239	1.11	2.78
Career	245	228	25	1516.0	1551	758	689	174	463	1161	100	68	0	15.4	.266	1.33	4.09

Randy Flores
Pitcher
Bats: Left   Throws: Left

	G	GS	CG	IP	H	R	ER	HR	BB	SO	W	L	SV	P/IP	BAA	WHIP	ERA
Season	65	0	0	41.2	49	29	26	5	22	40	1	1	0	17.9	.290	1.70	5.62
Playoffs	7	0	0	5.2	5	0	0	0	1	4	1	0	0	12.5	.238	1.06	0.00
Career	152	3	0	126.1	139	80	69	17	54	104	5	4	2	16.6	.284	1.53	4.92

Josh Hancock
Pitcher
Bats: Right   Throws: Right

	G	GS	CG	IP	H	R	ER	HR	BB	SO	W	L	SV	P/IP	BAA	WHIP	ERA
Season	62	0	0	77.0	70	37	35	9	23	50	3	3	1	15.1	.241	1.21	4.09
Playoffs	3	0	0	2.0	5	6	6	0	5	2	0	0	0	34.0	.455	5.00	27.00
Career	94	12	0	165.0	161	88	78	28	54	101	9	6	1	15.4	.252	1.30	4.26

Jason Isringhausen
Pitcher
Bats: Right   Throws: Right

	G	GS	CG	IP	H	R	ER	HR	BB	SO	W	L	SV	P/IP	BAA	WHIP	ERA
Season	59	0	0	58.1	47	25	23	10	38	52	4	8	33	18.2	.222	1.46	3.55
Playoffs	0	0	0	0.0	0	0	0	0	0	0	0	0	0	0	.000	0.00	0.00
Career	507	52	3	799.1	725	354	319	63	339	659	40	44	249	16.2	.242	1.33	3.59

Tyler Johnson
Pitcher
Bats: Switch   Throws: Left

	G	GS	CG	IP	H	R	ER	HR	BB	SO	W	L	SV	P/IP	BAA	WHIP	ERA
Season	56	0	0	36.1	33	21	20	5	23	37	2	4	0	17.3	.244	1.54	4.95
Playoffs	10	0	0	7.1	4	1	1	0	2	12	0	0	0	16.6	.148	0.82	1.23
Career	61	0	0	39.0	36	21	20	5	26	41	2	4	0	17.5	.248	1.59	4.62

Josh Kinney
Pitcher
Bats: Right   Throws: Right

	G	GS	CG	IP	H	R	ER	HR	BB	SO	W	L	SV	P/IP	BAA	WHIP	ERA
Season	21	0	0	25.0	17	9	9	3	8	22	0	0	0	15.2	.189	1.00	3.24
Playoffs	7	0	0	6.1	3	0	0	0	4	6	1	0	0	16.3	.150	1.11	0.00
Career	21	0	0	25.0	17	9	9	3	8	22	0	0	0	15.2	.189	1.00	3.24

Braden Looper
Pitcher
Bats: Right   Throws: Right

	G	GS	CG	IP	H	R	ER	HR	BB	SO	W	L	SV	P/IP	BAA	WHIP	ERA
Season	69	0	0	73.1	76	30	29	3	20	41	9	3	0	15.3	.277	1.31	3.56
Playoffs	7	0	0	8.2	9	4	4	1	0	2	0	0	0	15.2	.265	1.04	4.15
Career	572	0	0	607.1	617	270	241	46	213	374	34	32	103	16.4	.265	1.37	3.57

Jason Marquis
Pitcher
Bats: Left   Throws: Right

	G	GS	CG	IP	H	R	ER	HR	BB	SO	W	L	SV	P/IP	BAA	WHIP	ERA
Season	33	33	0	194.1	221	136	130	35	75	96	14	16	0	15.9	.289	1.52	6.02
Playoffs	0	0	0	0.0	0	0	0	0	0	0	0	0	0	0.00	.000	0.00	0.00
Career	194	137	3	910.1	948	507	460	130	352	552	56	52	1	16.2	.270	1.43	4.55

Mark Mulder
Pitcher
Bats: Left   Throws: Left

	G	GS	CG	IP	H	R	ER	HR	BB	SO	W	L	SV	P/IP	BAA	WHIP	ERA
Season	17	17	0	93.1	124	77	74	19	35	50	6	7	0	15.9	.327	1.70	7.14
Playoffs	0	0	0	0.0	0	0	0	0	0	0	0	0	0	0.00	.000	0.00	0.00
Career	199	199	25	1301.1	1326	638	594	137	403	829	103	57	0	14.8	.267	1.33	4.11

Anthony Reyes
Pitcher
Bats: Right   Throws: Right

	G	GS	CG	IP	H	R	ER	HR	BB	SO	W	L	SV	P/IP	BAA	WHIP	ERA
Season	17	17	1	85.1	84	48	48	17	34	72	5	8	0	16.9	.262	1.38	5.06
Playoffs	2	2	0	12.0	7	4	4	3	5	8	1	0	0	14.9	.163	1.00	3.00
Career	21	18	1	98.2	90	52	52	19	38	84	6	9	0	16.4	.246	1.30	4.74

Jeff Suppan
Pitcher
Bats: Right   Throws: Right

	G	GS	CG	IP	H	R	ER	HR	BB	SO	W	L	SV	P/IP	BAA	WHIP	ERA
Season	32	32	0	190.0	207	100	87	21	69	104	12	7	0	16.2	.277	1.45	4.12
Playoffs	4	4	0	25.1	19	7	7	1	11	13	1	1	0	14.7	.207	1.18	2.49
Career	317	301	15	1864.2	2029	1042	954	247	612	1048	106	101	0	16.1	.278	1.42	4.61

Brad Thompson
Pitcher
Bats: Right   Throws: Right

	G	GS	CG	IP	H	R	ER	HR	BB	SO	W	L	SV	P/IP	BAA	WHIP	ERA
Season	43	1	0	56.2	58	23	21	4	20	32	1	2	0	15.1	.267	1.38	3.34
Playoffs	4	0	0	2.0	3	3	2	1	1	3	0	1	0	19.5	.300	2.00	9.00
Career	83	1	0	111.2	104	45	39	9	35	61	5	2	1	14.6	.248	1.24	3.14

Adam Wainwright
Pitcher
Bats: Right   Throws: Right

	G	GS	CG	IP	H	R	ER	HR	BB	SO	W	L	SV	P/IP	BAA	WHIP	ERA
Season	61	0	0	75.0	64	26	26	6	22	72	2	1	3	16.0	.230	1.15	3.12
Playoffs	9	0	0	9.2	7	0	0	0	2	15	1	0	4	17.3	.194	0.93	0.00
Career	63	0	0	77.0	66	29	29	7	23	72	2	1	3	16.0	.231	1.16	3.39

Jeff Weaver
Pitcher
Bats: Right   Throws: Right

	G	GS	CG	IP	H	R	ER	HR	BB	SO	W	L	SV	P/IP	BAA	WHIP	ERA
Season (LAA)	16	16	0	88.2	114	68	62	18	21	62	3	10	0	16.7	.309	1.52	6.29
Season (STL)	15	15	0	83.1	99	49	48	16	26	45	5	4	0	16.8	.297	1.50	5.18
Playoffs	5	5	0	29.2	25	9	8	3	9	19	3	2	0	15.4	.221	1.15	2.43
Career	257	240	13	1568.0	1672	854	798	192	428	1044	86	101	2	15.9	.273	1.34	4.58

Brian Falkenborg		G	GS	CG	IP	H	R	ER	HR	BB	SO	W	L	SV	P/IP	BAA	WHIP	ERA
Pitcher	Season	5	0	0	6.1	5	2	2	0	0	5	0	1	0	17.7	.217	0.79	2.84
	Playoffs	0	0	0	0.0	0	0	0	0	0	0	0	0	0	0.00	.000	0.00	0.00
Bats: Right Throws: Right	Career	23	0	0	34.2	43	27	24	4	16	27	1	1	0	18.3	.305	1.70	6.23

Chris Narveson		G	GS	CG	IP	H	R	ER	HR	BB	SO	W	L	SV	P/IP	BAA	WHIP	ERA
Pitcher	Season	5	1	0	9.1	6	5	5	1	5	12	0	0	0	19.2	.176	1.18	4.82
	Playoffs	0	0	0	0.0	0	0	0	0	0	0	0	0	0	0.00	.000	0.00	0.00
Bats: Left Throws: Left	Career	5	1	0	9.1	6	5	5	1	5	12	0	0	0	19.2	.176	1.18	4.82

Sidney Ponson		G	GS	CG	IP	H	R	ER	HR	BB	SO	W	L	SV	P/IP	BAA	WHIP	ERA
Pitcher	Season (NYY)	5	3	0	16.1	26	20	19	3	7	15	0	1	0	18.9	.351	2.02	10.47
	Season (STL)	14	13	0	68.2	82	42	40	7	29	33	4	4	0	16.2	.308	1.62	5.24
Bats: Right Throws: Right	Playoffs	0	0	0	0.0	0	0	0	0	0	0	0	0	0	0.00	.000	0.00	0.00
	Career	252	238	28	1528.1	1701	881	830	196	519	918	80	96	1	15.6	.284	1.45	4.89

Ricardo Rincon		G	GS	CG	IP	H	R	ER	HR	BB	SO	W	L	SV	P/IP	BAA	WHIP	ERA
Pitcher	Season	5	0	0	3.1	6	4	4	1	4	6	0	0	0	29.1	.375	3.00	10.80
	Playoffs	0	0	0	0.0	0	0	0	0	0	0	0	0	0	0.00	.000	0.00	0.00
Bats: Left Throws: Left	Career	557	0	0	439.2	380	198	175	40	200	397	21	24	21	16.4	.233	1.32	3.58

Jorge Sosa		G	GS	CG	IP	H	R	ER	HR	BB	SO	W	L	SV	P/IP	BAA	WHIP	ERA
Pitcher	Season (ATL)	26	13	0	87.1	105	61	53	20	32	58	3	10	3	17.2	.298	1.57	5.46
	Season (STL)	19	0	0	30.2	33	18	18	10	8	17	0	1	1	15.2	.275	1.34	5.28
Bats: Right Throws: Right	Playoffs	0	0	0	0.0	0	0	0	0	0	0	0	0	0	0.00	.000	0.00	0.00
	Career	192	74	1	579.1	585	322	297	89	272	374	27	40	5	16.7	.262	1.48	4.61

HITTING

TB	CS	AVG	OBP	SLG	OPS
Total bases	Caught stealing	Batting average / On-base percentage	Slugging percentage		OBP + SLG

Ronnie Belliard		G	AB	R	H	2B	3B	HR	RBI	TB	BB	SO	SB	CS	OBP	SLG	OPS	AVG
Second Base	Season (CLE)	93	350	43	102	21	0	8	44	147	21	45	2	0	.337	.420	.757	.291
	Season (STL)	54	194	20	46	9	1	5	23	72	15	36	0	3	.295	.371	.666	.237
Bats: Right Throws: Right	Playoffs	14	50	2	12	1	0	0	4	13	3	6	2	0	.296	.260	.556	.240
	Career	1049	3812	528	1036	247	21	80	439	1565	379	576	32	24	.338	.411	.749	.272

Gary Bennett		G	AB	R	H	2B	3B	HR	RBI	TB	BB	SO	SB	CS	OBP	SLG	OPS	AVG
Catcher	Season	60	157	13	35	5	0	4	22	52	11	30	0	0	.274	.331	.605	.223
	Playoffs	3	1	0	0	0	0	0	0	0	0	1	0	0	.000	.000	.000	.000
Bats: Right Throws: Right	Career	518	1514	128	365	66	3	19	171	494	129	254	5	4	.305	.326	.631	.241

Chris Duncan		G	AB	R	H	2B	3B	HR	RBI	TB	BB	SO	SB	CS	OBP	SLG	OPS	AVG
Left Field	Season	90	280	60	82	11	3	22	43	165	30	69	0	0	.363	.589	.952	.293
	Playoffs	10	22	3	3	1	0	1	2	7	4	7	0	0	.269	.318	.587	.136
Bats: Left Throws: Right	Career	99	290	62	84	12	3	23	46	171	30	74	0	0	.358	.590	.948	.290

David Eckstein		G	AB	R	H	2B	3B	HR	RBI	TB	BB	SO	SB	CS	OBP	SLG	OPS	AVG
Shortstop	Season	123	500	68	146	18	1	2	23	172	31	41	7	6	.350	.344	.694	.292
	Playoffs	16	63	7	16	4	0	1	6	23	5	1	4	0	.338	.365	.703	.254
Bats: Right Throws: Right	Career	848	3338	498	945	138	18	27	254	1200	255	283	100	41	.351	.359	.710	.283

Jim Edmonds		G	AB	R	H	2B	3B	HR	RBI	TB	BB	SO	SB	CS	OBP	SLG	OPS	AVG
Center Field	Season	110	350	52	90	18	0	19	70	165	53	101	4	0	.350	.471	.821	.257
	Playoffs	16	52	8	13	2	0	2	10	21	10	16	0	0	.381	.404	.971	.250
Bats: Left Throws: Left	Career	1697	5907	1115	1709	380	21	350	1068	3181	878	1512	63	46	.382	.539	.921	.289

Juan Encarnacion		G	AB	R	H	2B	3B	HR	RBI	TB	BB	SO	SB	CS	OBP	SLG	OPS	AVG
Right Field	Season	153	557	74	155	25	5	19	79	247	30	86	6	5	.317	.443	.760	.278
	Playoffs	13	44	2	8	0	2	0	5	12	4	7	0	1	.260	.273	.533	.182
Bats: Right Throws: Right	Career	1181	4402	575	1184	225	45	147	620	1940	270	810	125	57	.316	.441	.757	.269

Aaron Miles		G	AB	R	H	2B	3B	HR	RBI	TB	BB	SO	SB	CS	OBP	SLG	OPS	AVG
Second Base	Season	135	426	48	112	20	5	2	30	148	38	42	2	1	.324	.347	.671	.263
	Playoffs	7	11	2	4	0	1	0	0	6	1	2	1	0	.417	.545	.962	.364
Bats: Switch Throws: Right	Career	376	1284	163	360	50	11	10	107	462	75	133	18	10	.322	.360	.682	.280

Yadier Molina		G	AB	R	H	2B	3B	HR	RBI	TB	BB	SO	SB	CS	OBP	SLG	OPS	AVG
Catcher	Season	129	417	29	90	26	0	6	49	134	26	41	1	2	.274	.321	.595	.216
	Playoffs	16	53	5	19	4	0	2	8	29	6	5	1	1	.424	.547	.971	.358
Bats: Right Throws: Right	Career	294	937	77	223	47	1	16	113	320	62	91	3	6	.291	.342	.633	.238

Albert Pujols
First Base
Bats: Right Throws: Right

	G	AB	R	H	2B	3B	HR	RBI	TB	BB	SO	SB	CS	OBP	SLG	OPS	AVG
Season	143	535	119	177	33	1	49	137	359	92	50	7	2	.431	.671	1.102	.331
Playoffs	16	52	11	15	3	0	3	6	27	13	10	0	1	.439	.519	.959	.288
Career	933	3489	748	1159	260	12	250	758	2193	493	394	36	17	.419	.629	1.048	.332

John Rodriguez
Left Field
Bats: Left Throws: Left

	G	AB	R	H	2B	3B	HR	RBI	TB	BB	SO	SB	CS	OBP	SLG	OPS	AVG
Season	102	183	31	55	12	3	2	19	79	21	45	0	0	.374	.432	.806	.301
Playoffs	6	6	0	0	0	0	0	0	0	0	3	0	0	.000	.000	.000	.000
Career	158	332	46	99	18	3	7	43	144	40	90	2	0	.378	.434	.812	.298

Scott Rolen
Third Base
Bats: Right Throws: Right

	G	AB	R	H	2B	3B	HR	RBI	TB	BB	SO	SB	CS	OBP	SLG	OPS	AVG
Season	142	521	94	154	48	1	22	95	270	56	69	7	4	.369	.518	.887	.296
Playoffs	15	51	9	14	5	0	1	2	22	5	7	0	1	.351	.431	.782	.275
Career	1393	5106	899	1454	356	30	253	954	2629	681	1041	99	39	.375	.515	.890	.285

Scott Spiezio
Third Base
Bats: Switch Throws: Right

	G	AB	R	H	2B	3B	HR	RBI	TB	BB	SO	SB	CS	OBP	SLG	OPS	AVG
Season	119	276	44	75	15	4	13	52	137	37	66	1	0	.366	.496	.862	.272
Playoffs	10	26	4	5	1	2	0	6	10	3	7	0	0	.276	.385	.660	.192
Career	1192	3676	486	936	211	27	115	518	1546	385	554	33	22	.327	.421	.748	.255

So Taguchi
Left Field
Bats: Right Throws: Right

	G	AB	R	H	2B	3B	HR	RBI	TB	BB	SO	SB	CS	OBP	SLG	OPS	AVG
Season	134	316	46	84	19	1	2	31	111	32	48	11	3	.335	.351	.686	.266
Playoffs	11	15	5	6	1	0	2	4	13	1	2	0	0	.438	.867	1.304	.400
Career	448	960	130	270	53	6	16	124	383	70	145	29	8	.331	.399	.730	.281

Preston Wilson
Left Field
Bats: Right Throws: Right

	G	AB	R	H	2B	3B	HR	RBI	TB	BB	SO	SB	CS	OBP	SLG	OPS	AVG
Season (HOU)	102	390	40	105	22	2	9	55	158	22	94	6	2	.309	.405	.714	.269
Season (STL)	33	111	18	27	3	0	8	17	54	7	27	6	0	.300	.486	.786	.243
Playoffs	13	35	5	7	2	0	0	2	9	4	7	0	0	.300	.257	.557	.200
Career	1083	3939	567	1041	218	16	188	663	1855	346	1068	122	54	.330	.471	.801	.264

Larry Bigbie
Left Field
Bats: Left Throws: Right

	G	AB	R	H	2B	3B	HR	RBI	TB	BB	SO	SB	CS	OBP	SLG	OPS	AVG
Season	17	25	2	6	1	0	0	1	7	3	9	0	0	.321	.280	.601	.240
Playoffs	0	0	0	0	0	0	0	0	0	0	0	0	0	.000	.000	.000	.000
Career	392	1227	164	328	56	4	31	137	485	119	302	25	8	.331	.395	.726	.267

John Gall
Left Field
Bats: Right Throws: Right

	G	AB	R	H	2B	3B	HR	RBI	TB	BB	SO	SB	CS	OBP	SLG	OPS	AVG
Season	8	12	1	3	0	0	0	1	3	1	13	0	0	.275	.449	.724	.265
Playoffs	0	0	0	0	0	0	0	0	0	0	0	0	0	.000	.000	.000	.000
Career	30	49	6	13	3	0	2	11	22	1	13	0	0	.275	.449	.724	.265

Hector Luna
Second Base
Bats: Right Throws: Right

	G	AB	R	H	2B	3B	HR	RBI	TB	BB	SO	SB	CS	OBP	SLG	OPS	AVG
Season (STL)	76	223	27	65	14	1	4	21	93	21	34	5	3	.355	.417	.772	.291
Season (CLE)	37	127	14	35	7	1	2	17	50	6	26	0	1	.306	.394	.700	.276
Playoffs	0	0	0	0	0	0	0	0	0	0	0	0	0	.000	.000	.000	.000
Career	260	660	92	182	38	6	10	78	262	49	122	21	9	.330	.397	.727	.276

John Nelson
Shortstop
Bats: Right Throws: Right

	G	AB	R	H	2B	3B	HR	RBI	TB	BB	SO	SB	CS	OBP	SLG	OPS	AVG
Season	8	5	2	0	0	0	0	0	0	0	4	0	0	.000	.000	.000	.000
Playoffs	0	0	0	0	0	0	0	0	0	0	0	0	0	.000	.000	.000	.000
Career	8	5	2	0	0	0	0	0	0	0	4	0	0	.000	.000	.000	.000

Timo Perez
Left Field
Bats: Left Throws: Left

	G	AB	R	H	2B	3B	HR	RBI	TB	BB	SO	SB	CS	OBP	SLG	OPS	AVG
Season	23	31	3	6	1	0	1	3	10	3	4	0	0	.286	.323	.609	.194
Playoffs	0	0	0	0	0	0	0	0	0	0	0	0	0	.000	.000	.000	.000
Career	574	1581	175	414	82	8	26	172	590	86	153	22	22	.301	.373	.674	.262

Mike Rose
Catcher
Bats: Switch Throws: Right

	G	AB	R	H	2B	3B	HR	RBI	TB	BB	SO	SB	CS	OBP	SLG	OPS	AVG
Season	10	9	0	2	0	0	0	1	2	0	4	0	0	.222	.222	.444	.222
Playoffs	0	0	0	0	0	0	0	0	0	0	0	0	0	.000	.000	.000	.000
Career	27	54	3	11	2	0	1	2	16	3	12	0	0	.246	.296	.542	.20

Skip Schumaker
Left Field
Bats: Left Throws: Right

	G	AB	R	H	2B	3B	HR	RBI	TB	BB	SO	SB	CS	OBP	SLG	OPS	AVG
Season	28	54	3	10	1	0	1	2	14	5	6	2	1	.254	.259	.513	.185
Playoffs	0	0	0	0	0	0	0	0	0	0	0	0	0	.000	.000	.000	.000
Career	55	78	12	16	2	0	1	3	21	7	8	3	1	.271	.269	.540	.205

Jose Vizcaino
Shortstop
Bats: Switch Throws: Right

	G	AB	R	H	2B	3B	HR	RBI	TB	BB	SO	SB	CS	OBP	SLG	OPS	AVG
Season (SF)	64	119	16	25	3	0	1	5	31	16	10	0	2	.304	.261	.565	.210
Season (STL)	16	23	3	8	3	0	1	3	14	1	4	0	0	.375	.609	.984	.348
Playoffs	0	0	0	0	0	0	0	0	0	0	0	0	0	.000	.000	.000	.000
Career	1820	5379	633	1453	204	47	36	480	1859	378	729	74	62	.318	.346	.664	.270

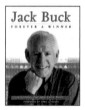
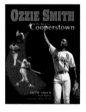

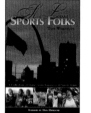